Will Cohu was born in Yorkshire in 1964. Educated at Exeter College, Oxford, from 1992 he freelanced as writer, editor and journalist, mostly for the *Daily Telegraph*. His books include *Urban Dog* (2001) and *Out of the Woods* (2007). His stories *Nothing But Grass* and *East Coast–West Coast*, were both short-listed for the *Sunday Times* EFG Private Bank Award. He lives in Lincolnshire.

WILL COHU

The Wolf Pit

VINTAGE BOOKS

London

Published by Vintage 2013

2 4 6 8 10 9 7 5 3 1

Copyright © Will Cohu 2012

Will Cohu has asserted his right under the Copyright, Designs
and Patents Act 1988 to be identified as the author of this work

This book is sold subject to the condition that it shall not, by way
of trade or otherwise, be lent, resold, hired out, or otherwise
circulated without the publisher's prior consent in any form of
binding or cover other than that in which it is published and
without a similar condition, including this condition,
being imposed on the subsequent purchaser

First published in Great Britain in 2012 by
Chatto & Windus

Vintage
Random House, 20 Vauxhall Bridge Road,
London SW1V 2SA

www.vintage-books.co.uk

Addresses for companies within The Random House Group
Limited can be found at: www.randomhouse.co.uk/offices

The Random House Group Limited Reg. No. 954009

A CIP catalogue record for this book
is available from the British Library

ISBN 9780099542353

The Random House Group Limited supports the Forest
Stewardship Council® (FSC®), the leading international
forest-certification organisation. Our books carrying the FSC
label are printed on FSC®-certified paper. FSC is the only
forest-certification scheme supported by the leading environmental
organisations, including Greenpeace. Our paper procurement policy
can be found at www.randomhouse.co.uk/environment

Typeset in Sabon by
Palimpsest Book Production Ltd, Falkirk, Stirlingshire

Printed and bound by Clays Ltd, St Ives plc

To my father, Tim, and for my son, Ralph

LANCASHIRE COUNTY LIBRARY	
3011812768678 4	
Askews & Holts	14-Oct-2013
942.846085 COH	£8.99
SEC	

Life, and Life alone, knows what is good for her children

Teilhard de Chardin

CONTENTS

I

SNOW

I remember first, before all things, the snow: how charming and voracious it was and how it transformed that Yorkshire landscape into a white canvas that both beguiled and terrified.

The snow came howling down the north end of Danby Dale and licked around my grandparents' cottage at Bramble Carr, jealously cutting us off from the outside world. Upstairs, crowded several to a bed and buried under piles of down quilts, we children watched by candle-light as the snow kissed the panes of the sash windows again and again, each time leaving behind the faint imprint of its lips, until the flakes began to stick and then, in a rush, smothered the glass.

Often, Bramble Carr Cottage was buried under snow-drifts. The back door opened on to a flagged passage beneath the slope of the garden, forming a weather-trap where snow piled up against the house, smothering the moan of the wind until the silence suggested we were far underground.

That back door opened inwards but stuck, something that my grandfather George never got around to fixing in the twenty years he lived there, despite my grand-mother's complaints. When the door was prised open, the compacted snow would stand stiffly on the threshold, waiting to be invited in before it would let us get out. With the passion of the blizzard gone, the snow had a different character; opaque, ambivalent, relentless, like some mordant relation who kept turning up at the door, year in, year out, to remind us where we came from and where we would end.

My memories seem to begin with that Yorkshire snow. I have a vague picture of myself lying in my crib, some washing flying in the wind and The Beatles' 'Yellow Submarine' playing on the radio. Then there is a gap and I am five or six and one afternoon I come walking out of the snow with my brothers and sisters, one of whom keeps losing her Wellington boots in the drifts. We are coming down the Fryup Road from Bramble Carr, heading to the Fox and Hounds to bring my grandfather home for tea. The snow has been ploughed and stands in walls either side, but more snow has fallen and drifted since. Our legs sink deep and our spirits vacillate between delight and terror. The snow has obliterated the landscape of moorland, hillside, pasture and drystone walls. From the windows of the cottage this sea of white appeared to be a thrilling new world without boundaries. In among the drifts the view disappears; the romance is clouded. Our boots are filled with meltwater and our gloves clotted with ice. The ploughed drifts tower over us like waves about to break; a flurry of snow thickens the encroaching dusk.

All at once, we are vanishing. The snow seems infinite

and indifferent to our anxiety and anger. We are half-frozen little attitudes of fear, on our way to becoming snow-children. Then, thank God, my brother John produces a torch. Its beam makes a hole in the night, showing the road going steeply downhill bending left then right until, spilling out across the snow, are the golden lights of the Fox and Hounds.

The latch clicks up. Inside the pub is thick with tobacco smoke and the smell of beer; low conversation rumbles like farm machinery. At one end, a fire is burning in a hearth with a black granite surround decorated with inter-locking hoops. I can see the flames through the legs of the men who crowd the place. Beer froth floats down from above. Hands pat our heads; a woman giggles. I hear the click of dominoes, the rattle of change, the rip of a match being struck and George's soft, guttural voice coming from the bar, where he is chatting to Bob Robinson, the local doctor. We need to go, but the pub is warm and comfortable, the more so for the darkness outside, and no one hurries to leave. We retell our walk to appreciative adults, and the purpose is forgotten in the pleasure of the story. Back at Bramble Carr, the food is getting cold, and my grandmother is getting cross.

The enduring affection I have for that childhood world is as much to do with its discomforts as its more relaxed passages. In winter there was always an element of difficulty to life at Bramble Carr, small challenges for the adults which, passed on to the children, created epic adventures. Nothing dangerous, just enough to give one a sense of accomplish-ment, a delight in solving familiar, manageable difficulties and a long-term habit of turning life's adult problems into a child's adventures, which is not always the best course.

The nearest shop, Gedge's, was a couple of miles away in Danby village and once Bramble Carr was snowed in, my grandmother would discover that there was an urgent need for basics. Dorothy was by this time in her fifties, not old, but five children and her constant dieting had taken a toll. The diets were arguably what killed her in the end. She hovered around the pantry when others sat to eat: 'I won't eat. I'll just have a Ryvita or two,' she would say, loading them thickly with Lurpak. She was elegant, poised and confident, but she was stout as George was lean and struggled to walk up the steep driveway in winter. The shopping was delegated to her grandchildren, who willingly took the sledge on fantastic polar expeditions, thrilled in the knowledge that buried beneath their feet were walls and streams. When the sun was out, that beautiful snow, white and crisp on top, creamy underneath and spread in superabundance was a confectionery delight to wade through.

Sometimes the weather was so bad that George would have to go to Gedge's. The worse the conditions, the more demanding Dorothy would be. She seemed unaware of the effort involved in mounting a foraging expedition, which required boots, sticks, sledges and sweat. Even George, who never swore and expressed displeasure only through a throaty 'harrumph', could be reduced to breaking point and once, very publicly, told her to fuck off when he had spent a morning sledging to and from the shop for supplies, only to be told to go back through the blizzard for another tin of Kitty Kat.

Harsh winters shaped the local temperament. The neighbouring moorland farms were always ready for snow. They

4

were built in close huddles, the sandstone farmhouses near to the dairies and byres, the humans wrapping themselves in the warm fug of their animals. Moorland farming was a tough business. Farms were small and unprofitable and mostly run by one man and the snow made the job impossible, but even so, farmers still talked about the winters of the past with respect, even affection. Many of the farmers came from families – Raws, Fords, Tindalls and Thornalleys – who had farmed the area for hundreds of years, and for them trial-by-blizzard was a rite of passage. In any case, an easy life never made for much of a story. The years passed, one after the other; you spent your life up to your knees in muck and if it wasn't for reckoning the intervals between the bad times you'd scarcely know what year it was.

There were winters in the late 1940s when the farm lads were sent out to search for sheep with broomsticks lashed together to make ten-foot probes and knew that they would still not reach the bottom of the drifts. The winters seemed to become milder by the 1980s, but they were still bad enough for Frank Raw, who farmed in Fryup Dale, to lose twenty sheep in one blizzard. He had a thorough look for them and poked about with a pole knowing that sheep can live a while under the snow. It seemed they had vanished entirely. The sun came out; the snow thawed and then it froze hard. When Frank stopped to ask some hikers on Glaisdale Moor if they had seen any sheep, he didn't at the time realise that the strays were under his feet, suspended in a snow-filled hollow, suffocated beneath a thick sheet of ice. Twenty frozen sheep in one shallow hole.

There were harsher places to be than Danby. Blakey Ridge, a few miles south across the moors, near the long gouge of Rosedale, is the most exposed spot in the area. In summer the moorland looks bald and leathery as worn hide and the wind blusters in your ears. Up the top is the Lion Inn, an old pub said to have monastic roots, now a warm refuge for cold walkers, a bowed and low-ceilinged building, grimly whitewashed, with windows little more generous than portholes in a ship. The Lion was the first pub run by John and Ilsa Kenney who later had the Fox and Hounds near my grandparents.

On Blakey Ridge they were snowed in from December through to March. Ploughing was futile: the drifts sprang back. John and Ilsa retreated to a world of candlelit silence, spending the dark afternoons by the fire, sleeping to the lullaby of the wind. Rescuers were a nuisance, since they always needed looking after once they got through. When their daughters Liz and Jane began to miss so much school they were considered feral, Ilsa rented winter quarters down at Hutton Le Hole and left the pub to her husband. John's passion was for military memorabilia. With Ilsa out of the way he settled down to solitude, waiting for spring while he set about polishing his collection of cap badges. He had two thousand cap badges.

Eventually, the thaw came, with a vinegary vegetative smell that prickled the nose. Water began to run into the stone trough that stood halfway down the drive to Bramble Carr. The snow became ice, slush, ice again, slush again, changing from powder to sheets to boulders, pebbles and puddles, leaching with a gurgle into the peat and heather and dead bracken and escaping down the moorsides into the tumbling becks. The air shivered with the thin, plaintive sound of lambs.

Just before the snow burned off the moors it looked

from a distance like a thinly stretched pallid membrane. Through it patches of grass shone glossy green: the smell of peat rose up from the warming ground. It was possible to imagine that this membrane of snow would split and immediately give birth to summer, so that we could pass straight from the sledge to the cricket field without having to live through the dull days in between. The snow was missed and hunted down by the children. There were sheltered places where it would hide for weeks even after the sun was out, old quarries on Danby Rigg or the over-grown little cut leading from the Fryup Road to Dennis Gray's cottage at High Bramble Carr. It was fun and at the same time sad to poke a bit of snow, like prodding a washed-up jellyfish. There was always a snowman or two on Fold Green, opposite the Fox and Hounds, little snow caricatures with button eyes and stick hands, slowly melting into formless clods.

Those snowy childhood winters were the beginning of my love affair with the North Yorks Moors. The love persisted down the years and, as happens, the lover became so entwined with the beloved that I fancied I had left much of myself there among the snow and the heather.

When I was younger I often went back to walk up Danby Rigg, the moorland spur overlooking my grand-parents' house, to sit and look down at the Dale enjoying the sense of self-affirming possession; this place was mine. It was always in my memories and my dreams; it was my happy place. In time, that selfish affection had to bend to reality; my life didn't turn out so simply as I hoped. When the snow of childhood melted I began to see the complexity of the landscape that had so inspired me. I had to reinvent it in order to explain myself. I still loved it, if anything more deeply than before, but I saw and appreciated its shadows as well as its glorious panoramas.

When I began this book I intended it to be something like a painting; a thoughtful, allegorical landscape perhaps. Posed against the purple romance of the heather-covered moors would be my grandparents and other family members. My grandparents would be holding hands and standing next to them would be a row of happy children, but there would be a questioning element in the background presence of my uncle Robert, who died tragically aged just thirty-eight, and there would be dark colours in the margins of the painting: the black of burned heather and troubled, oppressive skies as well as the low, rich sunlight of the north. The landscape would be littered with pagan burial howes as well as the stone crosses the monasteries left behind. There might be other mysterious elements, too; a storm-shattered oak and in the distance, a fiery volcano; in the foreground, a fish-tank.

Some of that design remains. But in the course of writing about the past, I was sometimes overwhelmed by the present. Three days after I began the book, my mother had a near-fatal stroke, and she was still recovering when my father was diagnosed with the cancer that would swiftly kill him. When I handed in the first draft, it was on the same day that I filed my divorce papers. The list of losses reached almost grimly comic proportions; even both my dogs died, including my talisman, Parker, who had, with my assistance, been an author himself and wrote a newspaper column for five years, which had kept me very nicely. All this passed in a two-year blur that left me in a constantly shifting state with regard to my material. At times I felt tentative, at other times too rude, so hard was I trying to keep myself separate from the book. In the end, I had to acknowledge that the contents of the book were playing a major part in what I was experiencing, so I allowed the past and the present to have much more of a conversation than I had intended.

What emerged was still that romantic painting, but I was much more present than I had intended, and the book had become more of an enquiring love letter to my grandparents, my parents, my family and my uncle Robert. It is still, as I had always intended, a gift of thanks to the people of Danby. Most never knew the significance they had for me, but none of us are owned wholly by ourselves.

2

THE MOORLAND SALON

Despite its name, Bramble Carr Cottage was not some quaint ancient dwelling, but a compact dressed-sandstone late-Victorian house, the junior relation of a much more splendid, sprawling place that was tucked behind yews the other side of a steep drive framed by pendulous syca-mores. Somewhat confusingly, this big house was known simply as Bramble Carr, as was the collective area it shared with the cottage. When people referred to Bramble Carr, they might have meant one house or the other, so the inhabitants of the cottage had their status enhanced by their proximity to their grand neighbours. 'Carr' has Norse connotations of swampland so the area had a damp history and both houses probably belonged to a genre of dwell-ings that had no productive purpose and were built because of the romance of their settings.

The cottage still sits at the north end of Danby Dale, though much improved since my grandparents' day. Over it broods Danby Rigg, one of those long, bony sandstone-and-heather fingers that extend outwards from the palm-shaped interior of the North York Moors. The sprawling villages of Danby and Castleton are close by, but the house looks hidden and secret, tucked away off the road that leads up though the straggling hamlet of Ainthorpe, over Danby Rigg and into the green depths of Fryup Dale.

My grandparents moved to Bramble Carr in 1966. Their previous home, at Hutton Lowcross on the fringes of the moorland town of Guisborough, was built in red-brick to their specification, with four bedrooms and a rudimentary central heating system. Bramble Carr had three meagre bedrooms and a bathroom scarcely big enough for Dorothy to conduct her toilette. Downstairs, there was a kitchen and pantry, a cramped dining room and a sitting room where Dorothy taught the piano. Under the stairs was a small lavatory that smelled of lavender air freshener and George's pipe-smoke. There was a storage heater in the kitchen. Upstairs there was no heating except electric blankets and an electric fire that stank of burning fluff. The windows were often blind with ice.

In retrospect, the move to Bramble Carr seems perplexing. George was a plant manager for Imperial Chemical Industries at Billingham, near Teesside, a short drive north from Guisborough. By moving to Danby he put twelve additional miles of high, cold moorland between himself and work. With its shops and buses, Guisborough was more convenient for Dorothy who had never learned to drive. She did once try a driving lesson and was going steadily across the moors until out of the gloom, detaching itself from the substance of ancient life, came a horned sheep. It stood on the road in diabolic silhouette; Dorothy screamed in horror and never got behind the wheel again.

When they decided to move from Hutton Lowcross, my grandparents had looked at places that were not so lonely as Bramble Carr, but Dorothy was infatuated. Bramble Carr took a hold on her heart. She had, she wrote to her children, seen the daffodils in bloom, heard the gurgle of water in the stone trough on the drive and sniffed the peat and bracken in the wind.

My grandparents did sometimes seem awestruck by their surroundings. The roads on to the moors were marked with cattle grids and the noise as you drove over them delineated the passage from one world to another, from the green to the brown, from the shade of pines and sycamores to a world where only a stunted rowan or hawthorn broke this glassy, curving landscape of the afterlife. No matter the conversation or small quarrel in hand, George and Dorothy would fall silent as they passed on to the moor. Perhaps they were struck dumb by the question that bleakness asked: where has everything else gone? Or, on summer evenings, perhaps they were revering the lurid beauty, as if they had travelled through space to find themselves hovering above an alien atmosphere flaring with cobalt and crimson. Perhaps they were pondering their decision to move. It was to prove rash, almost witless in the way it exposed them to each other.

The kitchen at Bramble Carr Cottage had rush matting and a blue Formica-topped table where George sat doing *The Times* crossword, a half-pint of home-brew at hand, a plume of St Bruno above his head. He never had a pipe out of his mouth. Dorothy smoked too, cigarettes or small cigars, leaving them in her mouth and letting the ash grow long as she painted moorland scenes. She was a self-taught artist, instinctive and bold. She used pastels and watercolours but liked oils best. She enjoyed the feel of oil paint; it went on thickly, physically palpable, like icing stained with poisonously beautiful Prussian blue or burnt sienna. Her small, intense paintings of horizons smouldering with autumnal hues hung above the few things of value that were squeezed into the small house: a walnut and rosewood dining table; a mahogany corner cabinet; a military chest; a pretty mirror.

While George did the crossword, Dorothy would hover by the pantry, observing her Ryvita diet or sit on the storage heater, warming herself. She baked beautifully: bread, sponge-cakes, Bakewell Tarts and rice cakes. The smell of flour and butter rose on a sweet layer of yeast leaking from the pantry where my grandfather's beer, made from Geordie Brew kits, bubbled in dirty pop bottles that exhaled gassy sighs, echoing my grandmother's complaints about her back, her legs and that sticking door. From time to time, a bottle would burst, sending the cat scuttling from the pantry shelf where it sat, dipping its delicate black and white paws in the goldfish bowl.

As a child I never wondered about where my grandparents had come from: George and Dorothy were a natural part of the moors. To my mind, they had never been children but had walked out of that landscape fully formed. Later, I assumed that the cultural ease of their household showed that they had been born into a similarly comfortable, middle-class environment.

Dorothy's background was actually working-class Doncaster, from the sooty red-brick terraces of the South

Yorkshire industrial heartland. Her father, Willie Ellis, was a builder from a line of porters, house painters and manual workers. Though there were prosperous times, Willie had a weakness for the horses and for women that left the family playing social snakes-and-ladders. His wife, Annie Louisa, intelligent, bookish and socially ambitious, spent the latter part of their marriage dressed in mourning black, knitting and weeping.

Willie was also a self-taught musician who played the cornet and ran a silver band: Dorothy inherited her mother's love of words and her father's musical passion and showed great promise at the piano. She practised five hours a day, but there was no money to support her talent and at fifteen she was out of school and working in hotels.

George's father, Joe Brooks, was a self-made man, a corn merchant from Worksop in Nottinghamshire, just down the road from Doncaster. Joe came from an austere farming background in Lincolnshire and had no time for culture. Dorothy once gave her father-in-law a book about local country houses. 'Thank you, Dorothy,' said Joe, gravely, 'but I already own a book.'

George's mother, Florence, was also from Lincolnshire farming stock. She was softer than Joe, but was devoted to making sure that everything was just as her husband required. Life revolved around the master of the house. George, I later learned, hated his silent, buttoned-up father, and could barely bring himself to go to Joe's funeral.

George and Dorothy had complementary good looks that endured into middle age. Tall, lean and broad-shouldered, George had striking hawk-like features and brilliant blue eyes. Lurking beneath his clipped moustache was a big, sensuous mouth. Dorothy was a bonny

Doncaster lass, a buxom beauty, with soft, creamy skin and an overt awareness of her blousy charms. In early photographs of them, they look tactile and at ease with each other. There was desire, but their relationship developed around their mutual love of the arts and music in particular. At Bramble Carr, there was always classical music, from the radio or from the piano when Dorothy was teaching or George was hammering away at a Beethoven sonata.

At times, the kitchen was a little cultural salon, which is – I think – what Dorothy had wanted to create, a small piece of Bohemia in a cold part of Yorkshire. Art was for her the means to self-expression, which was the greatest gift one could give a child. Sitting around the kitchen table, she treated her grandchildren as equals, showing us how to draw, humming Mozart until we recognised fragments, and pushing books our way. At seven or eight, I had a strange reading list: *The Lancashire Witches* by Harrison Ainsworth, the successful but now forgotten contemporary of Dickens, who specialised in lurid historical pageants; *Lorna Doone*, the Devon romance by R.D. Blackmore; thrillers by Frederick Forsyth and poems by Walter de la Mare. My favourite books were the mystic works of T. Lobsang Rampa, the Tibetan monk who later turned out to be a West Country plumber called Cyril Hoskin, who had never been to Tibet, but claimed that he had been taken over by the spirit of a monk after falling out of a tree where he had been photographing an owl. Mystic and fraud were equally fascinating, the more so for being the same man.

George and Dorothy had five children, three daughters and two sons, with eleven years between them. Their eldest was my mother, Muriel, always known as Mu, born in 1937. She married my father Tim Cohu when she was twenty-two. Dad was just three years older than her.

Within eight years my parents also had five children, three sons and two daughters. I was the middle child, born in 1964 at Hutton Lowcross: before me came my brothers Nicholas and John and afterwards my sisters Mary and Lucy.

Dad was a Royal Air Force officer, so we led a peripatetic life throughout the late 1960s and early 1970s. My parents were constantly on the move between married quarters. The RAF had a smoothly shrugging way of dealing with domestic baggage, and when quarters were not immediately available the wife would be expected to find somewhere to live with the children while the husband was put up in the officers' mess. Often this meant a prolonged stay at Bramble Carr, which my mother did not mind, since the marriage was volatile and she was frequently glad to get away from Dad who drank too much.

My mother's siblings were also occasional visitors to that moorland salon. Aunt Mary, two years younger than my mother, was nursing in Australia in the 1970s, but from time to time reappeared and walked huge distances across the moors on a quest to find the ideal pub. Rose, six years Mum's junior had, like her, married into the RAF. Rose seldom came to stay; she thought Bramble Carr was cold and haunted.

My uncles, Bill and Robert, were then young men in their early twenties. Both were in the merchant navy. Bill, like Mary, had settled in Australia, so we rarely saw him but Robert was often at Bramble Carr and left traces of himself about the place: his clothes, his music cassettes and his books. There was a folksy but psychedelic flavour to his musical tastes: Cat Stevens, Simon and Garfunkel, Steeleye Span and lots of Pink Floyd.

The uncles came home late at night, unannounced, climbing in the windows even if the door was left open as if emphasising their position as buccaneering outsiders. In the early morning, the presence of Robert or Bill was indicated by a sour mixture of cigarette smoke, sweat and beer, which could be traced to a sleeping bag on the floor of the sitting room.

My brothers and I particularly liked Uncle Robert. He was just a kid, a huge playful animal and closer to us than he was to the real grown-ups. You could do naughty things to Robert. You could jump on him when he was sleeping off the beer of the previous night. You could put soap on his toothbrush and switch his matches for joke duds. He took it all in good humour. He admired cheekiness. In contrast, when we did the dud match trick on my father, he looked tearful with rage, striking match after match with shaking hands. He did not like to feel he had been duped, and he roared at us. Robert roared, then gave us a pound and told us to piss off and buy some toffees at Gedge's – and get him some fags while you were at it. He liked boys to be wicked.

My brother John and I tested this good nature. We stripped the wrapping from Robert's chewing gum, doctored it with a layer of Imperial Leather soap studded with pepper, and carefully replaced the foil. He chewed a lot of gum to cut down on the fags, but in practice he chewed a lot of gum and smoked a lot of fags, so when he had finished a fag we brought him his gum and watched delightedly as his face registered an expression of intense disgust. Then came the roar, some appreciative laughter and the pound reward for being wicked. The results were so interesting – as well as profitable – that we thought we'd do it again. This time he chased us around the garden, still in his underwear, and it was slightly scary. Fortunately he ran out of breath.

Robert popped up regularly in our young lives and we always looked forward to seeing him. It was good to have an easy-going male in the family. Dad could be charming and affectionate, but he was much too young when he had children, and we brought out his own child-like needs. He sometimes seemed uncertain as to how many of us there were and what we were named. He often called me Lucy, the name of my youngest sister. He counted the biscuits, suspecting that we might be getting love or food that should be his, and sulked when my mother fussed over us. When he was sober he lost his temper, and was afterwards remorseful and perplexed at himself. When he was drunk, he could be outright nasty. My mother was apprehensive when he was around, and that nervousness rubbed off on the children.

In the way sons do, I still adored my father, the RAF officer with his glowering bad-boy looks and at primary school drew pictures of him in his uniform, adding crossed cavalry swords on his kneecaps to show that he was especially brave. But Dad struggled to relate to his young sons and it was hard to talk to him. He was, I think, not only jealous of our relationship with Mum, but scared of what we thought and felt about him.

There was no such complication with Uncle Robert. He would talk about anything. If you had fallen foul of the adult laws he'd tell you some story of his junior crimes – 'I used to go around Guisborough of an evening chucking bricks through windows' – and describe the joys of spending months sailing a ship of Brylcreem to Saudi Arabia. He'd give you a pound or a fiver or a tenner, or twenty. He kept pace with inflation.

I suppose, looking back, there was something unhealthy and compulsive about his behaviour, even in the early 1970s. He seemed to bloat and shrink in size according to his booze intake, and he had a greedy way of smoking cigarettes, one after the other, sucking at them until they burned red hot. Once I remember my mother pointing out to him that he had a lit fag in each hand. But you didn't think very much of health in the 1970s and there was no orthodox male beauty by which one might have judged his physical state. A tight, white rollneck sweater that showed off your beer-belly was good enough in those days. Everybody smoked.

At Bramble Carr, I was aware that there was a parallel adult world of secret things that could be pieced together from bits of odd behaviour, which, like persistent scratching behind the skirting board or the creaking of a floorboard in the night, might have a perfectly ordinary explanation, or might be signs of trouble.

A grown-up disappeared for a day or so: a phone call was taken in private. George drove off for a few hours; Dorothy abruptly took to her bed with a bad back. But the welcome difference between Bramble Carr and our own domestic set-up was that it was discreet. There were no raised voices, no parental rows, and no threat towards the children.

The only serious argument I remember was over the

business with Robert and the so-called tomato plants. Over the other side of the drive, the big house at Bramble Carr had been bought by a couple called Lyons. He was a director at ICI, which was a mixed blessing for my grandparents, since George was modest, middle-ranking and shy of self-promotion. Dorothy had more social ambition than George, but they were never close friends with the Lyons.

May Lyons, the wife, restored the gardens around the big house and, as help, employed a couple of former ballet dancers, housing them in a bungalow converted from a garage. My grandparents liked artists of any sort and had good relations with the dancing gardeners. Uncle Robert became friendly with them too. In fact, he spent a lot of time with them, helping them water the tomatoes in the greenhouse. Several bunches of aromatic, wilting tomato plants were hung to dry in my grandparents' pantry, then disappeared in the aftermath of an evening of acrimony.

Since public arguments were unusual and it was rare to see George wrathful, I asked Aunt Mary what had happened. Mary was over from Australia and had spent the afternoon down the Fox and Hounds, so she was feeling forthcoming. 'Well, the thing is, my dear,' she said, 'some grown-ups like to smoke a little something to help them relax, Robert was drying a bit of the stuff he likes to smoke in the pantry and Pa didn't like it, because it's not allowed over here. So Pa told him he had better get rid of it or the law would come. That's it, my dear.'

George was livid about Robert's admission that he had been colluding with the dancing gardeners in the use of May Lyons' extensive greenhouse. May had watered his marijuana plants herself, since they were hidden behind her tomato plants. George ordered the plants to be removed and drove them to a spot high above Fryup, on the New Way, and chucked them into a ditch. The incident was soon recycled for its comedy. It was funny, I heard it said, since George was after all a chemical plant manager. Years later, after Robert's death, I remember hearing that Robert had ten grand's worth of dope growing in the greenhouse, a huge wad in the 1970s. He was going to sell it on board ship. Somehow that stopped me laughing.

Dorothy's infatuation with Bramble Carr benefited others more than it did her. Her grandchildren in particular did well out of her romantic attachment to the moors. In my memory, it seems that there were years of happiness at Bramble Carr, though it can only have been a few seasons in the 1970s. Winters were high points, but during summer the children could live outside. We pillaged the garden and driveway for adventure, then crossed the tumbled-down drystone walls, moving up on to Danby Rigg, lost in the bracken that had invaded the lower slopes or falling into gullies and rabbit holes. Sometimes there were three or four of us, not so much a crocodile of children as a kind of segmented insect, crawling busily up and down the moorside. My brother John would be at the head, followed by me and Mary with our youngest sister Lucy bringing up the rear, clutching a dolly and tearfully determined not to be left behind, though she was only five or six. There wasn't much of a motive for the expeditions. Just going there and back and laying claim to the space in between. We were seeing how far we could stretch that invisible, elastic thread that connected us to home.

To our great delight we discovered that up the back of

Bramble Carr was a farm that was run by its animals. The cows queued peaceably in the yard, waiting to be milked at machines that puffed and squelched by themselves. On the ramp of the dairy, twenty cats lapped milk from a gutter, and from every stable door and barn poked curious noses, sniffing at us. It all happened under the sharp, laconic eye of a collie, sprawled in the dust.

Rowantree Farm was a magical place, which we reasoned must belong to a sorcerer. This turned out to be Bob Tindall, who, in typical Dales fashion, ran the small farm almost entirely by himself and was so busy and omnipresent that he was scarcely to be seen. He and his wife Brenda had three sons who were happy to have some company. Bob and Brenda often used to offer us tea: in fact, we hung around waiting to be asked. A Yorkshire tea with scones and cakes and sandwiches was not to be sniffed at. Not that the food at Bramble Carr was bad, but with Mum and Dorothy in the kitchen, there was likely to be a lot of talk and food could be slow to appear. Also, Dorothy got distracted when discussing music. Once she tipped a load of Vim in the soup, mistaking it for salt. She served it up anyway.

Rowantree had a squat and solid Georgian farmhouse with the usual complement of well-worn outbuildings. Over it hung the sweet smell of fermenting muck, milk and silage. There was an open midden in the yard, into which my sister Mary fell. She was drowning in the cowshit when John hauled her out. It was a narrow escape, but no one suggested we should not go back to the farm.

We found irrefutable proof of weird moorland inhabitants. On the top of the rigg were ancient burial mounds, which we knew, from reading Tolkien and Alan Garner, housed wraiths. About a quarter of a mile up the rigg was a hunk of weathered granite known as Fat Betty. There were other stones called Fat Betty in the area, but this was the one that mattered to us. Fat Betty had magical properties: the stone drew all living things to it and could provide protection to those who worshipped it.

Past Fat Betty wove a well-worn path that looked as if it was a series of huge interlocking footprints that might belong to the local version of the sasquatch. We danced around Fat Betty singing 'Oh Fat Betty, oh Fat Betty, please save us from the moorland yeti.'

At dusk we came off the moors. When the shadows crept over the heather, the rocky outcrops became fluid with darkness. They seemed to move and murmur; the ancient moorlanders woke up. That elastic thread pulled us back to the lights of Bramble Carr.

In the winter of 1971, when I was seven, we walked out of Bramble Carr through the snow drifts to begin our journey to Italy. My father had been posted to the NATO headquarters in Naples for two and-a-half years. We landed in sultry Mediterranean weather, nervous and tired. Dad took us for a pizza. The first words of Italian I heard my father say were 'Sono molto arrabbiato' meaning that he was very angry with the bill for the meal.

One of the unspoken attractions of Bramble Carr was the fact that Dad was rarely there. I assumed he didn't come because of work, and professed to miss him, but the truth was that George never liked him much and discouraged him from coming, and while I missed a father, it wasn't my father I missed.

George did not dislike Dad just because he had taken

away George's languidly beautiful, daughter, but because he lost his temper and hit his kids. My uncle Bill remembers seeing my father corner me in the garden at Bramble Carr and lay into me for some small misdemeanour. Bill told him to let me alone: when he was a boy Bill had been besotted by my father who had seemed to him the epitome of military gallantry. He was shocked to see Dad be so bullying with his children. I do remember how I flinched instinctively around Dad when I was small, expecting a clip around the ear. My aunt Rose says that George felt so strongly about my father he told her not to let him in the house.

Yet when Dad was happy, his good humour and emotional generosity were infectious. He would put on Beatles records and dance with my sister Lucy, swinging her round. He read us bed-time stories and made *The Wind in the Willows* come to life with different voices for Ratty and Mole and did a particularly convincing Badger. During summer holidays he took his sons sailing and fishing, played cricket with us and dragged us off to search the hedgerows for edibles. He had an obsession with foraging (his favourite book was Richard Mabey's *Food For Free*), which came partly from a love of nature and partly from his conviction that he could not afford to feed us all. Although he was rarely altogether relaxed, until he had a drink in his hand, he was better with his children when Mum wasn't there. She saw herself as our protector but he saw us as rivals for her affection, so when she interposed herself between us and him it only made him more resentful.

In Italy we lived outside Naples, between the sea and a dormant volcano called Monte Nuovo. Formed in the sixteenth century in a pustular eruption that swallowed the neighbouring villages, the mountain had grown thick with Mediterranean pines. If I pushed a fist through the carpet of needles and into one of the holes that dotted the mountain sides, I could feel warmth deep in the earth. Wisps of smoke issued from the ground and trailed away through the trees.

The area was part of a vast volcanic caldera, a collapsed crater, most of which lay under the Bay of Naples. Caldera are subject to a particular phenomenon called bradyseism, in which the collapsed ground can rise and fall under the variable pressure of magma. While we were in Italy, the nearby town of Pozzuoli – which had once been submerged under water – rose the better part of two metres.

Concrete and tarmac stretched and cracked and the ground was thick with Roman artefacts the earth had regurgitated. The other side of Monte Nuovo was Lake Avernus, Virgil's gateway to the dead. The Sibyl's Cave was a short drive away and down the road the underworld bubbled to the surface in Solfatara, a low volcanic crater alive with mud pools, exhaling steam-jets laden with sulphur. The smell carried for miles. The floor of the crater was hot enough to melt the soles of your shoes.

The locals were olive-eyed with angular faces, hooked noses and chins. Their skin looked black: they seemed African, not European. They were not conventionally good people, but equally villainous and loving. My parents knew mechanics, Communists and grave-robbers. People came to our house in the night with hessian sacks of loot, smiling crookedly at the door. They offered my parents Roman statues and vases; my father paid them with quarts of Chivas Regal and cartons of Marlboro.

Quite a few of the artefacts turned out to be fakes. The grave-robbers, who were complicit, were mortified and brought us a cockerel in a sack as recompense. We called it Henry Kissinger, because he was in the news. It strutted up and down the garden of our little villa, crowing, until Dad strangled it. We knew he had killed it, but he didn't tell us that that scrawny chicken he insisted we had for supper was Henry. It was Dad's foraging instinct, I suppose.

Kids could go anywhere in Naples. The worst that could happen was that you got your cheeks pinched. I spent my days roaming the mountains behind the house. My brother John broke into empty houses. My sisters played with the local ruffians. School did not seem to be obligatory.

The city smelled of drains and garbage. Students piled up old tyres and set light to them on the approach to the NATO base. I heard something about the Red Brigades: the Soviet Union was behind it all. 'That Harold Wilson is evil,' my mother said as she chased the cockroaches from our villa. They were the size of matchboxes, lived down the loo and flew out at you. News of Britain's collapse drifted through on the World Service: strikes, debt, stridency. But I could smell the heather and the wet through the radio, and despite the fun of Italy, I was homesick.

Italy was like my father: good-looking but combustible, with bright light and deep shade. The sunlight felt unremitting. I had to squint to see through the Mediterranean haze and houses, cars and people wobbled in the hot air that radiated back from the ground. In August, the humidity left me gasping. From our garden we could look out to the Bay of Naples. The sea was placid and brilliantly blue, innocent as the strokes of a child's crayon, but when you got down to the beaches you'd find yourself swimming against an incoming mass of turds.

My parents had some of their best times in Italy but Dad was still a party animal and drank. There was generally a row when my parents came home late at night. I'd be awake in the heat, listening for the key in the door, then hearing the music of their arguments: the low, steady andante of complaint, the broken arpeggio of someone trying to explain themselves, the canon of mockery and self-justification and an atonal finale of shouting and slamming. Mum disapproved: Dad was aggressive. It didn't matter which way round it happened, the result was the same.

The next day they would shut themselves in the bedroom, do whatever they did and be all right again. Parental relationships were difficult to understand. In public they agreed on little. Since I knew nothing about sex, I hadn't a clue what actually held them together.

It was bright and vivid and yet I wanted to be on the damp and clouded edge of the moors, where George would be sitting at the blue Formica table doing the crossword and Dorothy would be playing the piano or showing us how to use paints and the two of them scarcely exchanged a word. That was the kind of love I wanted, not this edgy stuff, where it was all one way or the other.

My grandparents turned up in Naples in their blue Renault, having driven all the way from Yorkshire. It was unnerving to see them. I was worried they might not be there when I got back and was quite relieved when they left. They belonged at Bramble Carr, for me. There I would always be safe.

3

ROLES REVERSED

In a portrait of George and Dorothy's children taken in the early 1950s, my mother, still a schoolgirl but only a few years off marriage, lurks at the back, her face misted over with melancholy and disdain. At the time she had fallen in love with horses; she looks like a sulky foal.

Next to my mother, my aunt Mary leans as if she might topple over with boredom. In the corner of the picture, little Rose smiles brightly. Sweets were being traded for smiles. Uncle Bill is at the bottom, chewing on his lip, looking at the photographer with mean calculation. To the fore is a beaming toddler, pushing his way into the camera's eye, one shoulder dipped. It is Robert, burly in sweater and bib, bursting with curiosity and affection.

It is the earliest picture of Robert: the same boy is recognisable in the last picture that was taken of him in September 1986. He stands in the doorway of a kitchen in Australia, again with one shoulder dipped, head slightly to one side with the same off-balance charm of that toddler, though he is not leaning forwards into the camera, but edging out of the kitchen door. He is just thirty-eight, but he has a snow-white beard.

A few weeks later, he killed himself.

Families deal with tragedy in different ways. In some a press conference is called while parents take questions; in others a parent slips into the bedroom one evening and has a word, or suggests a walk and a quiet chat. In our family there was a coded method. At periods I was informed of all the ailments of my parents' friends, but quite unaware that my mother or father was concerned about their own health. It took me a while to work out that if there was the rumour of disaster far away, there was probably real anxiety at home. It was not that pain could not be faced, but the idea of it had first to be introduced.

In Robert's case, the signs of trouble were more subtle because an opaque curtain had fallen between my mother and her siblings. She was trying to hold together a malfunctioning family within the strictures of RAF life. Robert had moved to Australia around 1980. There, Bill and Mary lived in country shacks or on huge seas, valuing experience above possessions; by 1983, my parents had only just bought their first house, where Mum had tried to smooth Dad's rough edges by creating a home full of antique glass and pictures, as if the fear of breaking things of value might curb his temper. She could only bear so much. In retrospect the picaresque details of Robert's life that filtered through to us – the restlessness, the tender yet unaccountably broken relationships – were symptomatic of her need to manage his story in some optimistic way.

His death sounded almost gentle. The news was broken to me, not by my mother, but my eldest brother Nick, who told me over a few drinks that Robert had killed himself because he had been unwell for a while. Nick made Robert's suicide sounded almost inadvertent: an impulsive action taken in a bad moment. I accepted this. It was impossible to think of Robert being depressed, that big loving bear who we had adored. Suicide was not unheard of in our middle-class world, but the one or two people I had heard of who had killed themselves had been described by my parents as weak, hopeless cases, which I felt Robert was not. Moreover, there was a social stigma to such tragedies. If a member of a family killed themselves, clearly there was by implication something not right with the family: the weakness might be contagious. So suicide was not talked about.

The real grief took time to travel from Australia. It arrived, my mother told me, years later, one afternoon when she was standing over the sink. She experienced a wave of desolation and almost fell over. There was a tree outside the kitchen window, a huge lime, with a bird feeder on it. She saw the birds coming and going busily and had an awful sense that life itself had died suddenly a long time ago but was still going on, stupidly and implausibly.

Suicide often destroys families. It refutes the emotional hold of the living, denies their own existence and is the most aggressive act that can be undertaken by someone who perceives themselves as being at their lowest ebb. When someone who is loved prefers oblivion to love, you wonder, what did they learn about love? The empty space becomes an articulate, demanding ghost. For a few years, Robert's death was simply moved to the margins of my life. Then, for the first time, my own emotional world turned strange.

On a damp October morning in 1990, twenty years on from those first snow memories, I woke up on Danby Rigg with a hangover, looked down at Bramble Carr and wished there was someone who could tell me what to do with my life. The previous evening, I had got drunk and then driven all the way from London up to North Yorkshire, pursued by a horrible emotional vacancy which I hoped could be banished if I visited the place that had always seemed so emotionally coherent.

There were reasons to be in that state. I was twenty-six and working for a big theatre as a producer and director. I had got out of my depth and no longer knew what I was doing. I saw my contemporaries suffer similarly and pick themselves up – for some, loss of confidence was as common and temporary as a cold – but I fell into a hole of miserable introspection and self-doubt from which even my common sense could not drag me. Dishonesty was the word that kept coming to mind. I was dishonest. Every word I spoke, every gesture I made, seemed false: the only real thing was the pervasive interior blackness.

I crumpled into this void. I knew it was wrong, but there was nothing of any counterbalancing significance. Not even affection, or good news. The light had just been turned off. Work had its pressures, and then there was my drinking and the dope, too, but the real catalyst for this collapse was a bad love affair. In retrospect the details seem gruesomely comic: at the time, it was in every way painful.

I had become involved with an actress with an ex-boyfriend who did not share her sense of an ending. A few months into the relationship, I began to pass blood and ended up in hospital. My girlfriend was concerned that she had given me an infection – though tests later showed this was not the case. However, by then she had followed the doctor's advice and contacted her ex. She doubted his fidelity; perhaps he had caught something which he had given to her which she had then passed to me, the innocent party. She was angry with him, but afterwards, things became unsettling. The former boyfriend vanished from his home: there were phone calls at odd hours. The girlfriend thought she had seen him in the street near her house. She was afraid, she said, then, abruptly, she dumped me and eventually went back to him.

It was a shock. I took to obsessively considering the comic ironies of the situation, unable to believe the betrayal. This was not how things were supposed to happen. How could the person I knew do this? Perhaps I had not known her; perhaps all that I thought I knew, all that she told me about her feelings, was an illusion. The doubt spread into other areas of my life. Then came that sense of falsehood.

Within weeks I was as the ex had been, a wretched mess, turning up unannounced on her doorstep, hopelessly asking for the return of things she did not possess, principally my sense of self-esteem. A reversal of roles had taken place. There were ostensibly good and sensible reasons she had ended the relationship, to do with work, and her needs versus my needs, but I felt that ultimately, I had inadvertently brought them back together. I was not the lead in her play: I was a supporting role.

The night before I drove to Yorkshire I had met up with her, but the evening had gone wrong. Why was I, the person who had seemed so necessary just a short while before, no longer required? How had I disappeared? Where the hell could I find those bits of myself again? She didn't know. Why should she? Stuff happened. Things were complicated. Have you ever loved two people? She just wanted to go home.

This time, as I sat on Danby Rigg and looked down over the Dale, there was no sense of things being in the right place. I did not understand myself: how I could have so little control over my feelings? Was I in love with this girl? Is that what this was about? There was no conventional love in those emotions: they were freezing waves of deprivation that seemed to have absolutely nothing to do with the person who had sparked them. When would I feel better? In my condition the moors looked infinite yet claustrophobic. The romance of the place was mocking.

It was a long time before these feelings subsided. The abrupt withdrawal of emotional validation had let rip a lot of submerged feelings that I could not at the time attach to any source other than this failed relationship, since I had never considered that I might have anything significant hidden away. The loss of control destroyed a certain blindness that was required to function day to day in the theatre and eventually I left it. In the end, this was a good thing, but for a while my interior world was alarming, not least my sudden interest in my uncle Robert. Since my own sense of invulnerability was now in tatters, I began to ask more about my uncle: this was typical of the family way. Rather than admit I had serious problems, I preferred to show a curiosity in others' tragedies.

My mother may not have known the words to say to me, but with great intuition she showed me a letter that Uncle Bill had written to her after Robert's death. Bill had grown into a tough but eloquent man, a merchant sea captain with a whiff of the pirate about him. He had a beautiful but tricky wife called Barbie; he liked women and was fond of the whisky bottle. When the booze took him, he could be insufferably argumentative and there was often a flurry of chaos around him. But he was a loving father with three gorgeous young sons, Joseph, Luke and Matthew, the latter a Bangladeshi orphan he and Barbie had adopted.

His letter to my mother was both a lucid account of his love for his brother and a forensic description of Robert's long descent into depression. I was shocked to discover that Robert's death was no spontaneous act: it was the culmination of a campaign to rid himself of life. Inside me, the landscape of my childhood shifted uncomfortably. How had it come about that my grandparents' youngest son, the big warm bloke, had turned into the kind of weak man who killed himself? What had been done to him? I remembered nothing dark in my grandparents' household: just the light of their affection.

I had last seen Robert in 1980, shortly before he moved to Australia to join Bill. It never occurred to me at the time that there was anything seriously wrong with him.

He was overweight and smoking heavily again, but that was typical of Robert. I was too young to know what trouble looked like.

4

A LOST NAVIGATION OFFICER

Associated Steamships Pty Ltd
SS *Wiltshire*
28th October, 1986

Dear Mu,

I have written a brief description of Rob's last year or two with us, so that you can get an idea of how it was for him and us.

It is very difficult to do this with any precision, as far more is always left out than is described. However, I bashed on with it as I felt it was important to pass on some stuff about Rob to both you and Rose. I typed it and photocopied it because my handwriting becomes quite illegible over a long time and because I could not face writing twice.

There was of course very much more than I have bothered to write and it wasn't by any means so obvious at first that Rob was on a steadily self-defeating path. Nor did he give up without a lot of fight. He kept trying one thing then another to make himself be 'normal' and enjoy life and make progress, but he never could keep going. I simply do not know the cause of this. For my part, I am sceptical of psychological explanations. I don't feel that his background was emotionally adverse enough to warrant his behaviour. I tend to feel more that in people like Rob, there is something fundamentally wrong with their brain chemistry or nervous system right down at the basic level. No matter what the environment, they just don't generate the same response to it. Rob himself, in our talks would often shout with frustration that he couldn't _feel_ this way or that way, as he was aware other people did. My problem, towards the end, was in trying to help him to do this. I felt confident at first that I could do it, but obviously I couldn't.

For those of us intensely involved with Rob over the last years, his suicide has been a shattering experience. Mary, Liz _____, Barbara and more recently, Judy, all had great involvement with him. For all of us there is left a sense of failure, no matter how unreasonable or illogical it is to feel it, and an emptiness which only Rob filled.

It was very good to chat to you Mu. I am glad that you are doing a bit of drawing again. Now that Tim has finished with the RAF, life may be a new thing for you both. I think you deserve a break, especially from the endless commitment to your family. If you want to know any more about Rob, my address is . . .

Love to Tim and you and family, Bill

Looking back over the past six years, it seems to me that there was always something wrong with Rob that we could not fathom out. When he arrived in Australia, he said he wanted to do any work other than seafaring. But he seemed to lack the ability to make the most elementary decisions to fulfil his own wishes, that is, he absorbed all suggestions put to him as possibilities, but did nothing about following them up.

He attempted to do contract clearing for the ACT Forestry Commission, but soon quit as it is hard and lonely work. He several times drove off on his own, ostensibly to simply find work and 'set himself up' but these expeditions always came to nothing. Mary said that he was once offered the job of exterior painting and maintenance of a set of holiday buildings owned by a friend of hers but he turned it down. He did try quite hard at times to push himself into accepting life and work on his own, but always sheered off at the last moment. He was very like a person fifteen years old – he wanted to be independent – but, to his chagrin, he found it a difficult and lonely business.

Because he was so lovable, with a dry sense of humour and infinite kindness, especially with kids, we all kept trying in any way to get his life going. We knew that he wanted to get up enough momentum to be able to carry on, on his own. He wanted only to be 'normal', to have a wife and some children especially. I don't think he ever quite realised that once having achieved these things, life's problems are not necessarily solved.

He spent most of his time alternating between Mary and Barbara and I. He was a delight to have around, very generous, quite good fun when he ceased worrying about himself, and hard working when one gave him something to do. The only thing was, he remained pretty well incapable of doing things for himself. Eventually, I got him a job on the *Roger Rougier*, a small coaster skippered by a friend of mine. This was not supposed to be anything other than stop-gap work to provide a decent income whilst he decided what to do with himself. I was always torn between offering such help, and thus being interfering 'big brother', or leaving him alone. The trouble with the latter approach was that, when left alone, Rob never did anything at all. He would worry more and more about himself, then eventually turn up with all his concerns and pour them out, virtually pleading for suggestions. It is very difficult when you do really love a person in this condition not to make as many helpful suggestions as you can.

When we moved to Tasmania, Rob followed us down, stayed with us for a short while then moved into a flat. This was a cheerful new place, easy to keep clean and pleasant to be in. He now had a paying job and a reasonable home. He soon added a girlfriend in the person of Liz C____. For a while he was happy, but as time progressed, things began to go wrong. I do not know the reasons why, except that they ran hot then cold about marriage, and she became pregnant by him but had an abortion. After his calamitous trip to England where they were to get married but didn't, the more serious depression began for Rob.

If one visited him in this period, it was usual to find him sitting morosely in a blue fug of cigarette smoke, his flat in a mess, endlessly questioning himself as to what was wrong about him. He spent more time round our place after this, and eventually declared he could no longer bear to live in his flat. It depressed him too much. He said he really needed a house, something he could commit himself to and which demanded his attention and involvement. Again, we fell into a set response. As he expressed repeated desire for a house, but day by day, week by week, did nothing at all to acquire one, we went into action to help him choose one. Eventually he did so, being as pleased with it as he first was with his flat.

We helped him set up home again and tried in every way to get him going. Externally, his situation was not at all bad. He was a very good-looking and eligible man, with a nice house, friend and relatives nearby, nephews and nieces who really loved him and good earning potential seafaring on the coast. To a hell of a lot of people, his circumstances would appear fortunate. But the trouble came from within. Left alone in his house, he fought hard to make a go of it but became gradually more sad and despairing about himself, convinced that he was a failure and that there was something wrong with him. He began visiting a psychiatrist. I spent (and still do) many futile hours wondering what is the secret of helping a person in this state. I loved him so much and felt sympathy for him. Some of the things he said, I find I feel myself, but only now and then, or to a lesser degree and not to the level he felt then.

Sometime after this, at Christmas time, he had himself committed to a mental hospital in Hobart (I was in Korea at the time) after declaring to Barbara that he simply could not go on. By this time he had tried treatment from a vitamin therapy specialist as well as the psychiatrist. He was not in the place for too long, and later declared that it had been utterly horrible and said it did him no good at all. He also said that he was so depressed whilst there that one day he waded into a swimming lake with the express purpose of drowning himself, but found this impossible to do. We did not take this story seriously. His fortunes took a further down-turn when the little coaster he was working on went broke and was laid up. This was only supposed to be temporary work, but Rob had not budged, even though he heartily hated the job by this time. I always felt faintly responsible for leading him into a situation he subsequently did not like, but if I said nothing, he did nothing.

I became angry. Nothing was any good, not the job, not any form of treatment, not the house (he now declared it a weight around his neck) and not his personal relationships. I declared myself bankrupt of suggestions, other than that I could get him employment in my company, working on ships again.

Rob took up this offer and at least managed to keep his head above water for a while. It was around this time that Liz M____, a good friend of Barbara's asked Rob out to dinner. The relationship took off like a rocket and all of us associated with them were utterly delighted.

Suddenly, one no longer had to worry how Rob was: he was happy. There is no doubt that this must have appeared as a magical granting of all his wishes. Liz M____ is an attractive, very intelligent lady with two teenage children. She lived in a very comfortable house, into which Rob moved in short time. She worked full time as an accountant, so Rob soon found he could be an invaluable help domestically, a situation that he loved. Within months, he was talking of marriage and of having a baby.

Rob was a totally giving man. He gave Liz and her two children all his time and love, which was considerable. It was clear to see the beneficial effect he had on the children. He once said to me that he enjoyed it all so much that he actually felt pleasure in cutting and packing their school lunches for them. During this time, he was as good as I have ever seen him – very happy. But the seeds of destruction were sown in him. Knowing him so well by this time, it was impossible not to think that his gnawing self-doubt would emerge in some form or other to frustrate him.

In the middle of last year, Liz sold her house and she and Rob and family moved into his house. I had been living in it for the previous few months as matters between Barbara and me had reached a critical point and we had separated. Everyone worked to get the house up to scratch for a whole family to live in it and I moved down to my girlfriend's place nearby. All was still going well for them, as least so far as we could see. By this time, Rob was working on my ship, an experiment we tried and both liked. However, we had got on to opposite swings, so that when I was home, Rob was at sea and vice versa.

When I next returned from sea, I found that the relationship between Rob and Liz was going wrong. Her husband had reappeared on the scene. I kept out of it, but I knew Rob would not have the resilience to take what was coming. He had bet everything on this, put all his eggs into one basket. Sure enough, the day came when he returned from the ship to be told it was all over and they would have to organise a separation. Rob was thunderstruck.

They carried on living together for convenience for a little while. One day Liz came down to see us to ask if we had seen Rob. We said we had not. She had not seen him herself for two days: he had not said where he was going. A day after that, he turned up, saying he had been walking in the bush to sort his mind out. Subsequently, I found out that he had taken a vast array of pills of all kinds and washed them down with whisky after driving himself into a remote area. He had come to after two days and staggered around in the forest for another, before being able to locate his car and get back home. He hid these facts from us for quite a while.

Before Liz left, and immediately afterwards, we all had long conversations with him at different times, trying to help him through his misery. In typical generous fashion, he had given most of his own basic furniture away before Liz moved in with all hers. Now his house was rather bare. I tried desperately to get him to set it up so that he could feel at least reasonable in it. We encouraged him to get a dog, together we steam-cleaned all his carpets and he bought a couple of good tables and set of very good chairs. I suggested that he took an extended holiday overseas to provide a distraction from his memories. He repeatedly kept saying that he was OK and not to worry.

Sometime after this, I went off to sea again, but Rob asked for time off work without pay after his leave expired. Judith, my girlfriend, was keeping in constant touch with him – we were all worried. After a few weeks, Judy phoned to say that she and two of our friends, Penny and Dick Smith, had found Rob in his bed in an absolute stupor. They managed to get him conscious enough to get him into the car and down to our place. It took twenty-four hours before they could get much sense out of him, but he was remarkably well again in two more days. He had taken God knows how many different pills of every variety,

and washed them down with whisky. He had been unconscious for three days when they found him.

This was a difficult time for Judy, as she had to look
after him as he returned to normal and of course listen
to his interminable self-berating and declarations of
uselessness. However, he made a rapid recovery and went
out to stay at Penny and Dick's place in the bush.

When I returned home, he had gone back to his place.
He swore that he had now got it all out of his system,
refused to even consider professional help. I frankly did not
know what to do about him. I kept giving him an ear to
talk into and shoulder to lean on, but secretly I guiltily
worried that I should be forcing him to get psychiatric help.
I just didn't have the heart to try and force him into it when
his previous record under treatment was so unsuccessful.

I should say that, in between these moments of high
drama, Rob was often surprisingly cheerful and good
company. I don't want to give the incorrect impression
that it was always gloom and doom. Most of the time he
went along reasonably well, some of the time quite positive, and so one would be optimistic that he was handling
his problems. Such optimism was a delusion however.

A little later, I was again at sea when Judy called me
to say that he had left a note wishing us all well and
vanished. I knew he meant business this time. I had myself
relieved on board and flew home at once. We mounted a
police search and went looking for him ourselves. We felt
we knew his pattern by this time.

After four days he returned, in the most terrible distress,
weeping continuously and declaring himself unable to love
anybody or even to kill himself. I brought him home to
our place at once. He had taken the tube of his vacuum

cleaner away with him to connect to his car exhaust but in four days had been unable to bring himself to do it.

He was a totally distressed man. I did not wish to part with him for a minute. He dreaded going to another mental hospital and I did not want to send him there, I wanted him home with me. I felt that, as nothing else had ever worked when he was down and out, the answer might lie in his being in a house with plenty of children, getting plenty of love and support and relaxing from serious life decisions for a while. I also felt that he would feel better if he was kept occupied, with less time for reflection.

We set about putting him together, starting with the smaller things. We joined a local gym and did a workout each day. We knocked off his whisky and tried to reduce his interminable cigarettes and endless cups of coffee. He and I systematically went through all his unpaid bills and financial matters, sorting it all out.

He picked up fast, even occasionally spending a bit of time laughing and joking. I remember pointing this out to him one day, but he quickly refuted it, saying it was all a façade and that he still felt totally blank inside. During this time he declared that he would sell his house as it depressed him madly to even go into it (he had said exactly the same about his flat).

I recommended that he rented it out, but he did not want to. I then offered to buy it myself, as I was looking around for one anyway at the time. We had three evaluations made and I paid him the mean of the three. I borrowed nearly all the money from the bank and paid him off. This allowed him to settle some of his debts as it was some time since he had worked.

Before he could return to work, the company required

a medical examination and a psychiatrist's report to say that he was OK. He took a further couple of months off work in an attempt to get sorted. We stored his fridge, washing machine and new table and chairs at Penny and Dick's. I kept him going to the gym: I got him to talk to me for hours about what was worrying him. We took him out and at the same time involved him in the running of the house. I encouraged him to make things and start small projects using the good-sized shed and tools that we have.

It was difficult. He could not run on his own much. Left to himself, he would often stop and smoke cigarettes and drink cups of coffee. After doing this he would nearly burst with rage and guilt at himself. Having listened to him a lot, his self-accusation began to sound like a pre-recorded speech. He would say the same things time after time after time. On each occasion I would try to lead him gently to realise that many of the things he felt were a distortion.

He would often agree, but a week later he would say it all again. It was impossible not to be irritable with him at times, and I'm sure he was aware of this. I feel grateful to Judy: it certainly was a bit hard on her, a tremendous responsibility especially when I had to go off to sea again.

Eventually, Rob got the necessary medical certificates and returned to work on *Goliath*, one of our ships operating out of Devonport. When he returned after eight weeks he seemed unusually cheerful. He was fairly positive about what he wanted to do. He said he was going to go up to Launceston and set himself up in a flat. I suppose I should have realised that this was a deception, but I believed it for two reasons. The first was that I desperately wanted to believe he was up to it and the second was that I knew that at some stage I'd have to back out and set him going again. Actually, I fell for it perfectly and was really pleased. I offered to come up and lend a hand to look for a place but he said he'd rather do it by himself. He had a cheerful dinner with us and a few beers: everyone was happy. He spent the night with us and the next morning, after giving us all generous presents, he left for Launceston, promising he would ring in a few days. I was so pleased with his progress that I phoned Mary to tell her, and we spent the next few days feeling better about Rob than we had done for a long time.

In the middle of the week we heard he had phoned Penny and Dick to enquire after his dog, which they were looking after. By the end of the week I was a bit anxious and cursing him for not phoning us as he'd said he would. On Sunday, the police reported finding his car empty and locked up, out in the countryside near Launceston. I knew at once what was happening, told them of his established suicide pattern and to search around the car.

They came back later and said that they had found him dead. He was two hundred metres from his car, naked and face down.

As the pathologist later gave the cause of death to have been alcohol and drug overdose combined with exposure and hypothermia, I feel he removed his clothes deliberately to ensure death.

He had taken a vast array of pills again, washed down with whisky. He had locked his car and sat smoking under a nearby tree, perhaps while the pills and whisky took effect. Eventually he fell face down and lay in a coma. It is thought that this was Wednesday 1st October. He remained alive for four days, dying in the early hours of

Sunday 5th October. This leaves the agonising thought that if only something had been done to locate him, or if the people reporting seeing the car had done so a day earlier, he could have been saved.

The coroner's clerk, a sergeant of police, was a sympathetic and understanding man with a vast experience of suicide. He took me to the mortuary to identify Rob. When I mentioned the thought about finding Rob alive, he said that it was his experience that no way had yet been found to stop a determined suicide, including the range of mental treatments.

When I am honest with myself, I have to admit that if we had found him, and he had come round in hospital to find he had to screw up his courage all over again to get away, he would not have thanked us. It must have taken immense determination to plan it as he did, having to deceive us who were fairly wary by this time, collect the various medicines and then go off alone to do it.

For my part, even if he did want to die, I didn't want him to.

I loved him, he was very big and friendly and open-hearted. I told him this but he seemed unable to believe it. I admired him in lots of ways, even though it was frustrating trying to get him going in life.

We had a small cremation service at Launceston crematorium. It was a perfect spring day and there were many brilliant bunches of flowers sent: they glowed in the warm afternoon sun. We were a smallish group, but quite a few children. All wept in the aftermath of the service. The minister seemed surprised at the emotion shown and said what a caring group of people were there.

I felt glad that Rob's view of himself, so negative, was thus proved wrong. It was obvious now at least, that he was a very lovable man. I remain bitterly sad that I was unable to communicate this simple truth to him.

His estate is in the hands of the Public Trustee, as he died intestate. I sorted through all his papers again (it was only six months or less since I had helped him put them all in order). He owed quite a lot of money on his credit cards, at punitive interest rates, while still having ten thousand dollars sitting uselessly in a non-interest bearing cheque account. He simply could not be bothered to transfer sums from one to the other.

The truth is that he had totally neglected everything almost immediately after he and I had got him squared away again. In all his possessions there is the same feel of gross neglect. Nothing appears to have had any real value to him; nothing is looked after or cared for.

A surprising number of people have expressed their condolences. Many seamen have done so, as well as astonishment that he should take his own life. That he was so well liked he never could see. It will be a long time before we get over losing him.

I shall bury his ashes in the beautiful forest at Penny and Dick's and plant a big strong tree over them. It is very peaceful there.

Bill Brooks
26/10/86

In the Australian National Library in Canberra, there is a brief entry by the Public Trustee: *Robert George Brooks* *of 21 Stephen Street, East Devonport, Tasmania, navigation officer & single man, died between 1st and 5th days of October 1986 at Cressy, Tasmania. The gross value of his estate was sworn under $61,109: probate was granted to the Public Trustee of Tasmania March 1987.*

Cressy is pretty farming land, quiet and rural. I had imagined that he had lain in the dry bush, but Tasmania is greener than the mainland. It was not, in any case, a particularly hot summer. That week the weather was cool and fresh, some rain, a north-westerly wind with patches of cloud. It was a busy week in Tasmania: everybody was looking out for Gordon Francis Curtis, one of Australia's more notorious murderers who had escaped from prison and was moving throughout the Tasmanian countryside. The headlines were all about the search. The solitary death of a lost navigation officer did not make the newspaper.

5

THE WOLF PIT

It had taken Robert six years of struggle to defeat himself and everyone who loved him. Even if he wanted to die, both body and spirit were opposed to his decision. This wasn't weakness, but a misapplied strength. He had been determined and deceitful.

At the time I read Bill's letter I questioned my interest in Robert. Besides the stigma attached to suicide, there was also a queasy glamour. I knew my experiences were not the same as Robert's, but I recognised something in what Bill described, some kind of thwarted emotional neediness; some kind of insatiable hunger.

Bill had written that Robert blamed their parents for his depression, but that Bill felt there was in reality something pathological about Robert's condition: such a deep depression must be a disease because it seemed quite disproportionate to any possible familial cause.

He was as right as anyone can be. There is no definitive reason as to why people collapse this way; we are subject to a multitude of potential influences. Genes, family, experiences and addictions all play a part. There are nobler analogies, but for me it's as if the psyche is like a carelessly managed garden shed, with a mass of forgotten old poisons and combustible materials lying around in dusty cartons. It's bucolic and fun until the packaging rots through and some unlucky chemical combination takes place.

It helps to know what you have stashed away. Twenty years ago, I knew surprisingly little about my family. Beyond those childhood memories of Bramble Carr, I knew nothing about my grandparents. I could not judge what influence they might have had on how their son turned out, and I did not feel able to question. Because of the oblique process of family discourse, I was worried that anything I asked my parents would have been seen as being implicitly about me, and have suggested some criticism of them.

Home was too tender to take that. There was sympathy if a child seemed unhappy when they were away at boarding school or university. My mother wrote anxious letters and promised to lavish food and affection on us when we came home. But, close up to their children, both my parents had a terror of emotional 'silliness'. There was a line beyond which they did not wish to venture.

This was odd, given that cultural values were prized in my parents' home as they had been at Bramble Carr. Emotion in art was laudable, but emotion in life was silly, yet my mother in particular was not insensitive. She could see when things were wrong, but did not know what to do. She had married so young; how could she have the answers?

Last year, after my marriage collapsed and my wife and I separated, I was going through boxes of old letters retrieved from the attic of our house when I came across a note written to me by my father after my drunken trip to the moors. I had ended up back at my parents', glossing over the true details of my experience, but obviously confused and depressed. I had stayed for a few days and made some telephone calls to square things with the ex-girlfriend.

In his brief letter, Dad wrote that he hoped I was 'more tranquil in mind than recently'. He regretted that he might have said a few unfortunate things – I had been given a warning not to be 'silly' – but it was only out of love, and added, which was the real point of the letter – that 'mother refuses to accept any blame for our forthcoming monster telephone bill. Since you did seem to hog the line last week, perhaps you could help out? Very much love from us both, Dad.'

The phone bill was one of the ways in which my parents waged their long and engrossing battle, in which there was all sorts of silliness.

I was left to make what I could of Bill's letter. The man he described puzzled me, as did my own emotions. The man I had admired as a kid felt a failure and had given up on life. I now felt as if I was sinking into failure – was Robert's story a map for my own future?

I read and reread that letter of Bill's and in the process a dialogue took place between myself and Robert. Perhaps it was the sheer concrete detail of Bill's description and his persuasive narrative. Once I had got over the generalised emotion that had conflated myself and Robert, I read the letter not as a personal message to me but as literature and I began to see not similarities, but differences.

Robert had approached death with the same resolution that others went about life, trying and failing and trying again. His was a shadow version of life. He said he wanted to be happy, but for him, that meant extinction: everything was expedient to this goal, even the love his brother showed him. I found that thought horrifying. Yes, I was like this man in my composition; he was family. But in our objectives I was nothing like him. Absolutely not. He wanted to die; I wanted to survive.

Ultimately, that bad romance did me a favour. It would not be the last time that I would experience that kind of chaotic emotion and sit on the Rigg looking for inspiration. But things were never so bad again, even in circumstances that were ostensibly much more complex. My feelings would not be so black; even when they were destructive, they always conveyed the message that I was alive. Bill's letter decided that for me.

However, the experience left me with the conviction that to understand myself I had to know a great deal more about my family. You can't have too much information. The unexamined past gathers a force disproportionate to its significance. It might be a threat, but it might also be a refuge and a resource.

High up on Danby Rigg, by the New Way, the steep road that climbs from Fryup Dale, is an ambiguous landmark known as the wolf pit. It was the local doctor, Bob Robinson, who first told me about it, twenty-five years ago, shortly before Robert's suicide. My grandparents were dead by then: I had finished at university and wanted to go walking, so I called Bob and Ruth Robinson who put me up at Ainthorpe House, one of those solid but welcoming Yorkshire places, built in sandstone with unfussy classicism.

Years before I had often visited their solemnly beautiful daughters. Dorothy would take me with her. She was teaching one of the girls the piano, and enjoyed a gossip with Ruth. There was a big Victorian dolls' house that we played with in the gloom of a cold, unlit nursery. I loved that dolls' house: it had everything in miniature, even a leg of lamb and a little girl doll in a pinafore. The house was otherwise unpopulated, but so realistic in every detail, from the maids' quarters in the roof to the mirrors and books in the parlour, that it was eerie with life. You scarcely dared breathe around it in case you missed the sound of tiny footfalls.

Bob and I looked at maps of the moors, while Ruth, grande dame of the village and tricoteur of Danby Tennis Club, knitted and smoked and talked without pause in her waspish way about the 'pinkos' who were invading the courts and how they might be guillotined. Bob paid her no attention as we discussed where I should walk. I'd never bothered with maps when I was young. We just roamed. Life now required plans.

I spotted 'wolf pit' written in the small gothic script that the Ordnance Survey uses to denote something of historical interest. Bob, who was an avid antiquarian and was always collecting material for a book he intended to write about the area, said that the wolf pit was a hollow in the moors which in the fourteenth century had been used to trap packs of wolves that roamed the area in cold winters.

Ruth remarked that a similar fate could be meted out

to the new round of incomers, the Johnny-come-lately upstarts and woofter academics. They could drive them on to the tennis courts, and let them expire on the tarmac they craved. Wasn't it in Burma that the Japanese had perished trying to take the tennis courts? Kohima? Bob? Bob?

But Bob was telling me about wolves and about the lolloping beast that an old farmer he knew claimed to have seen. There were occasional sightings of wolf-like creatures on the moors, sometimes when sheep were savaged, mostly explicable as dogs that belonged to visitors or had been abandoned. But there was this one farmer, not given to flights of fancy, who described a long lean creature he had seen slink down the moorside and make its way up the dale, weaving through the rocks and heather. Bob had asked him for more detail. 'I can't rightly say,' came the reply. 'Not a dog. It were a beast. And it lolloped.' Bob opened his hands to evoke the farmer's perplexity: 'It just lolloped. And then it were off.'

The description of the beast had a touch of the Baskerville about it, and yet, as the hound of Dartmoor had been just a painted dog, so this lolloping beast was not altogether fearsome. I could imagine it lolloping through the heather and over the rocks, loose-limbed, comically awkward, disinterested, a cartoon monster. But the image had its troubling aspects too: that something was funny did not mean it was not cruel.

That day I looked high and low for the terrible pit above Fryup, but there was nothing: just the sunlight coming and going over the purple moors, the honeyed scent of the heather flowers that were coming out, the sound of curlews and below, the lush, tumbling landscape of Fryup Dale. I had the disturbing sense that the place was fobbing me off with beauty and waiting for me to leave.

It seemed too soft and sensual. Where was the pit, the terrible pit that would bring meaningful shade to this summery opacity? Eventually I thought I had found something awful. A steep gash a few feet deep where the moor looked as if it had been split by an axe. Here, I thought: yes, here. This is where they came, driving the wolves with torches from Fryup and Danby and Glaisdale. I could imagine it: the fires moving over the moor at night, the baying of hounds. This was the secret, sacrificial heart of the place.

'I like the sound of that, but the pit is round, as I remember,' said Bob, nodding kindly, as if I was describing implausible symptoms. 'But there are dramatic landslips in the area. That's what you saw. The pit has changed a bit. Probably doesn't look as fearsome as it used to.'

It is easy to make too much of the past.

After many trips back, over the years, I eventually worked out that what was marked on the map as a wolf pit was also marked as an old burial howe. There, next to the side of the New Way was a heather-covered mound with a shallow green hole inside it, enough for a couple to curl up in, a lovers' bed perhaps, but not the dreadful pit I had imagined in which snarling creatures with pallid eerie eyes would stare up at their human captors, awaiting execution and weaving some lingering lupine curse.

The pit was other things to other people. Susie, Bob Robinson's daughter, told me that she remembered the pit as being huge when she was a child, though in the book he eventually completed, Bob himself said that the story was that they used to trap the wolves in the howe by projecting slabs out across the lip, so it was never very wide.

The historian Nicholas Rhea told me that he had seen the wolf pit marked on a map as Wolf Pit Slack, a trench that bridged the narrowest part of Danby Rigg. Were there ever wolves? Herbert Tindall, who farmed in Fryup, told me that when he was a child he had seen a book that had the whole story of the wolves in it, including the claim that the farm at Fairy Cross Plain in Fryup – an odd little hill where the wee folk are said to dance – was given by the king to the man who slew the last wolf.

The pit was, and is, many things and nothing at all. Behind the purple drama of the description is a subtle shade of ideas. If this grave was later used as a pit for trapping wolves, then it represented not a pit for sport or punishment, nor the place from which the wilderness emanated, but the place into which it was driven. The pit represented progress. That entailed the loss of wilderness, but it initiated in its place the romance of a name.

The place of horror turns out to be no more than a green scoop, sometimes shadowed, sometimes shining with the bilberries and grass within it, as if a mouth had opened from which streamed a beam of light. So Robert's death, which had looked from a distance to be an all-consuming tragedy was, close-up, the story of a man finding release from his pain and how his brother had showed such defiant love. The past was a grave, a trap – and yet, also neither of these. Just light, coming and going.

At the wolf pit you imagine you will stare into a hole

littered with bones, but what draws you to that place is not what you take from it. The wolf pit seems a delicate illusion. You walk towards it; there is nothing, just the curve of the moor; then it is a soft green light, and then it is nothing again.

6

DEPENDENCY

Driving to Danby on an autumn afternoon, I turned on to the moors after Guisborough, wound the window down and was thrown by the richness of the scents that a little warmth had unlocked. Heather and honey: bracken and bog. They reminded me of George and his St Bruno. Those twists of tobacco, tarry as oakum, rubbed between his long fingers. The smell of wool and sheep shit, the decaying sweetness of fermenting grass; a ruminant grandfather, a cud of tobacco.

The memory of my grandparents never disappeared after they were gone from Bramble Carr. It was diffused into the stuff of the landscape around them. That rich, dark smell of the peat evokes the mid 1970s, when I was eleven or twelve and at boarding school near my grandparents'; I spent a lot of time in their car while George drove me to and from school, smoking his pipe.

While my earliest memories of Yorkshire from the beginning of that decade are of uncomplicated happiness, the mid 1970s were more ambiguous. I was often alone at Bramble Carr which was less fun than it had been, but more generally, I was making the transition to adolescence and the adult world moved closer and looked puzzling. To my eyes, even Dorothy began to acquire shadows. In part it was because I was thrown into dependency on my grandparents.

My parents had come back to England from Italy in the spring of 1974. Dad was posted to Buckinghamshire. Like both my brothers, I was sent away to Barnard Castle School in County Durham, about sixty miles from Danby. Barnard Castle was then at the lower end of the private school menu, a rugged Victorian establishment in a brooding Jacobean-style building overlooking the Tees, next to the grand French folly of the Bowes Museum. The school was popular with parents who were in the armed forces. It was cheap, did not have any reputation for abuse and was strong on games.

I did a year at the prep school, Westwick Lodge, before going across the lane to the main school. Westwick Lodge was a sprawling Victorian villa with the modern dormitories and classroom block hidden at the rear. It had a long, sloping front lawn, thickly planted with shrubberies, where the boarding contingent played war, one group defending the house while the others attacked. Round the back was a playground and a muddy hill with a few trees. Here, too, one army of boys would defend the hill while the others launched frontal assaults. Front and back, day in, day out, the boys practised attacking and defending and falling over dead.

School showed the grown-ups in a bad light. We were told by the headmaster, Mr Marshall, that we were a family and he and his wife were our parents. They were decent enough, but it was the other members of the family that one had to watch out for.

My form master, John Hay, was a drinker with a furious red face, a yellow stained beard and mean eyes. 'Old Hay' had a musical voice, one of those lilting northern accents that came from the front of the mouth while from the back of his gullet he kept up a congested wheeze. He was a whacker with an armoury of tools. He favoured a two-foot aluminium ruler, which called his 'chatter-checker.' At times he also used a rubber hose that he kept near the fish-tanks down the side of the room. There were whackings for doing things, whackings for not doing things or for not adequately doing things, for not trying or for trying in the wrong way. There were also whackings for no reason the boys could understand – and they did try to understand.

The boys were immensely patient with their persecutor. They would wonder what it was they had done to displease him, or debate whether he himself was in a good way; perhaps he was tired, or fed up or possibly drunk. Grown-ups were always drunk in those days.

Old Hay had the knack of making you feel sorry for him. Even at the moment of public humiliation, as he was about to whack, you would feel you had let him down and the sting you felt was shared – that it was even inflicted on him. One's hatred for the man could not eradicate the desire to be loved by him, the sense that he was owed for the effort he was making to school you.

He wore old wool sweaters and cords and drove a motorbike to work, coming into class in his boots and biker's waterproofs. It was said that he had been in the Army in the war, that he lived somewhere up in the wastes of Teesdale, that he had a brother with whom he had bitter fights which were the cause of those scars on his face. Each half-truth one heard about the outer man added to the conviction that the inner man was some kind of antique beast. The Army part would make some sense. There were lots of men who found their way from the forces into the classroom, carrying with them obscure lessons they had learned in the war.

Much of the day he sat at his desk, smoking or cleaning his pipe, breathing short and sharp, his thick shaking hands fiddling with fishing flies. He hummed to himself, his eyes squinting with amusement. He held his class in his hand, wound them tight with terror and released them with a joke directed at one of his whipping boys. 'Nice is a nasty word,' he said. 'Got is a horrible word. Don't shake your apostrophe pepper-pot over your work. And do your flies up. The birds are hungry this time of year.'

If you felt miserable the thing to do was to get up early and go down to the kitchen where you would find Mrs Marshall stirring a vast vat of porridge. She would give you a cup of tea and tell you not to think of yourself as unhappy because, if you did, you will only make yourself unhappy. Look at the things there are to enjoy! And don't sit there reading. Why don't you go and pretend to get killed like all the others?

My objective was not to die, not even in play. I intended to run away to the moors. I fantasised that at night I would sneak off to Bramble Carr and climb into the pantry window to steal whatever cake Dorothy had been making. In time they would realise that I was there – the Police would come looking – but they would hide me in the garden shed.

A boy called Crozier, a popular, freckled, good-looking boy, found me looking sorry for myself around the back of the school block.

'Honestly. It gets easier,' he told me. 'Don't worry. Term comes to an end. Nothing goes on for ever. Not even Old Hay.'

I was grateful for his words and appalled at what happened next. During a reading period in class, when we were supposed to be absorbed in our books, Crozier put up his hand to ask if he could go to the loo, and was denied. He asked again, shortly afterwards, clearly desperate.

Old Hay put aside his pipe and the fishing fly he was working on. He made Crozier wait, while he stood, stretched, grinned and chuckled and ambled down the side of the classroom where the fish-tanks were. He picked up a jug of water. 'Have you heard of the Chinese water torture?' he asked raising the jug high and allowing it to flow slowly into the tank. The water purred down, in a thin, soft stream. Boys laughed and then went silent, shifting uncomfortably on their seats. The water went on and on. He was going to stop soon, wasn't he? But he continued to pour, watching Crozier from the corner of a half-closed eye.

Crozier's face turned red and he bowed his head in humiliation. Under his desk formed a puddle of piss.

'Oh dear. 'Ow sad. Never mind,' said Old Hay. 'Better fetch a mop.'

I wrote home and complained about Old Hay. The staff read our letters and told my parents I was a bookish sort and had a tendency to exaggerate. My parents were sympathetic to me, but they had been brought up to trust

authority. The school was a family and protected its prod-
igals. Old Hay watched me slyly, tapping his chatter-
checker on his hand. I was not the only one to speak
about his methods. The whackings eased off. I noticed
that around the Marshalls, Old Hay was a different person
– stooped, beard-tugging, soft-spoken, deferential and coy.

When I saw him abasing himself this way, I felt strangely
disappointed. It is tough to see your despot grovelling for
his job. You need him to stand up for himself. It was a
curious sort of dependency, but one that I suppose is
common in relationships that are based around fear. If he
was really such a pathetic man, how could he exert such
control over us?

George and Dorothy took me away for weekends and
half-terms. I looked anxiously for their car on those
Sundays when we joined the main school boarders in the
big chapel, sitting separately in the organ-loft and looking
down on our future life, on the rows of boys in herringbone jackets and blazers. When George and Dorothy came,
she sat next to me, her calm bulk moving with the music,
so warm that she seemed to heat the whole loft. When
she sang, the dust danced in the sunlight to the hymn tunes
running through her.

The road to Bramble Carr went east towards the industrial belt of Stockton-on-Tees before striking south on to the
moors. Sometimes George took a different route, through
Kildale and Commondale, up via Castleton. This way, the
moors came into view with a gentle leavening of the horizon.
There were markers: the bent park railings in Kildale,
stooping trees behind them and beyond a glimpse of the
hump of Roseberry Topping and the obelisk of the Captain

Cook memorial, high on the hillside. After this, the land turned darker and the features of houses and roads and trees leached out. I watched, anxiously wondering when we would be safely in the moors.

It took an hour and a half to drive to Danby and fuel was costly. Sometimes my grandparents just took me out for lunch or tea. One evening we bought fish and chips from a shop on the Horsemarket in Barnard Castle, sitting in the car to eat them. The rain lashed down and the streets had a sleek black winter gleam. It was distinctly a northern town: it had wide market spaces, cobbles, big merchants' homes and crouched, tight-squeezed stone terraces. There was little light in any windows as if it was too precious to spill. A few people walked quickly and furtively home, processing one by one into a funnel of darkness.

We listened to Radio Four while we ate. There was a bit on the news about *The Exorcist* which was released in England that autumn. I had seen a poster for the film in a shop window; it had a disturbing image of a cross. The news said a boy had killed himself after seeing the film. There was a discussion; it was just a film, someone said. It was evil, said a contradictory voice. There were things that you simply did not show on screen. It was diabolic.

The blue Renault filled with the smell of vinegar. On my parents' book shelves I had found copies of books by Dennis Wheatley. There was a lot of the Devil about in the 1970s. People had little beards and clomped around in hard-heeled boots like goats' feet. Dorothy could sense my discomfort.

'There are nasty things,' she said. 'But if you don't see them, they can't frighten you.'

Was it as simple as that? If you did not see a problem, it need not trouble you? I tried to believe her. I wanted to trust Dorothy. She was my exorcist. I needed her to give the darkness what for, in her black coat and hat, little bag on her arm, cameo brooch on her breast. But I knew that what she said was not true. Nasty things did not go away because you ignored them; they gained in power. They needed to be talked about and reduced with conversation. Dorothy would talk about most things: was there something about the supernatural that troubled her? Perhaps she was afraid of the idea of there being a darkness deeper than the winter night we sat in.

It was not until many years after my grandparents died that I could bring myself to visit their graves in Danby churchyard. I simply did not wish to think of them as being dead.

The churchyard sits among the fields midway up the dale, a neatly walled citadel of evergreen introspection. Tall Irish yews shelter the grey church. To east and west the dark riggs rise; the wind comes off the moors, striking whispers from the neat rows of headstones that mark generations of Tindalls and Raws. From the graveyard, a net of stone walls reaches out across the dale to the moors, joining the living and the dead.

My grandmother's gravestone is on the south side of the church, in a patch left long with wildflowers over the summer. She had wanted to be cremated but George had her buried and then he was buried next to her. He did not want a memorial, but the anonymity of his plot seemed unfairly dismal, so in the end my aunt Rose had George's name engraved on Dorothy's stone. There they are, organised by the living into a resemblance of how they had slept in life, him on the left of the bed. All that is lacking is the Teasmade.

When I first visited, she had a gravestone but George had nothing. It made me think that even in death she had a compelling mass that dominated the relationship. Looking back to those schooldays that I spent at their house, I think the sense of security she gave me was complicated. I was drawn to her in expectation of more than she could give. She had her own neediness, and at the centre of the gravitational pull she exerted was a black star.

She was by then physically inert and did not go outdoors much, partly because of her weight and her bad back; but her relationship with the moors was more ambivalent than it had been. She admired the world outside, but as her sighing indicated, it did not cheer her. She appropriated the landscape as an emotional vocabulary and eliminated the need for real contact with it. Her paintings were almost always moorland scenes of lurid introspective drama, thick oils that verged on the abstract in their depiction of the wilderness. The wastes existed in her heart and mind, with their glorious panoramas of repentant purples and effulgent sunsets.

She exhibited with success and sold many of her paintings, but a few remained with her children. One hangs in my uncle Bill's house in Victoria, Australia. It is an oil of a moorland landscape under dark skies. There a storm-shattered oak in the painting, which in a conventional landscape might be at the left of the picture, framing the eye's passage across the moors. Instead, the tree is slap in the middle of the canvas. It is Dorothy, I think, this tree. The painting says: 'Look at me in my ruined majesty.'

There was no counterbalancing weight in the household. George had no gravitational pull. He was amiable, sceptical and sometimes smug with his occasional barbs. But he was discreet about his thoughts and conspicuously undemanding. He made instant coffee using water from the hot tap rather than boil the kettle.

I had struggled badly with maths at school, largely through terror of being punished for failing. George gave me a book of maths problems, full of questions about firemen filling buckets with leaks and boats travelling with broken sails. I liked this sort of thing and George put aside *The Times* and pushed away his glass of beer to make room for me next to him. He was patient and gentle.

'Let us first consider what is known to a certainty,' he said. 'And then let us see what we can discover from that.'

At these times, I remember that Dorothy seemed slightly put out. George liked solving abstract problems, but not the sticking back door.

It was inevitable that Old Hay, the jovial, sadistic teacher would become the most influential figure in my life; I had nightmares about the man. But Dorothy also had a pull on me. I had supposed that she and Old Hay were opposites, one light and one dark, the exorcist and the demon. But they were not so far apart. They both had the weight of disappointment inside them.

Those days spent by myself at Bramble Carr were very quiet. I rummaged in the attic looking through the boxes of books, the piles of my uncles' possessions, the sextants and uniforms left from maritime college. I thought about going up on the moors by myself and possibly running away so that I would not have to go back to school. But I was wearing grey shorts and a school sweater and the green damp of the stone walls would mark them and I would get in trouble. The truth was that I had become fearful of the moors: the night streamed down from them as if from a black glacier. I preferred to curl up with a book in the corner of the dining room.

Alone with my grandparents, I realised that they didn't talk much any more. George might open a bottle of Hirondelle in the evenings, but the wine rarely made things lively. They shared the odd joke. People with names like Winterbottom would make them laugh, as did the sign at a supermarket saying Customers' Rear Entrance. Otherwise, George could be silent for hours at a time.

One Saturday, when George and Dorothy were due to go out, a black and white television they had borrowed from friends was put in the spare room. My parents had only just got a television and the most marvellous things on it were the commercials: Brazilian Blend is everybody's cup of coffee; I'm a secret lemonade drinker; happiness is a cigar called Hamlet. The programmes were less inter-esting. That Saturday night there was a choice of football or Val Doonican singing. Neither was Dorothy's taste, I thought; she was only interested in culture. But she came and sat with me, fascinated. We watched the football, then Val Doonican. Her face relaxed and a small smile played on her mouth. I was allowed the electric fire on. The room smelled of burning fluff. Dorothy was sleepy. George called her from downstairs. It was time to go. She sighed and went, then popped back, with her bag and coat, and stood watching for a few minutes, while George called again. She had been devoted to art and books and Beethoven, but if she needed more Val Doonican there was obviously something trivial lacking in her life.

Quite soon I did see some nasty things that I couldn't pretend did not exist. A day boy at the prep school told a small group of us that his father had some pictures we should see. He had found them in the loft. In those days, such things were kept in the loft, rather than on a hard-drive. His father was a doctor and the boy reasoned that he had the pictures because they demonstrated certain strange things that bodies did.

He showed them to us, as we huddled around the doorway to the outside loo block, fingers nibbled with the cold, legs blue in our shorts. I was apprehensive about seeing the pictures, as it was not my strategy to draw attention to myself but the boy had delivered his side of the bargain by bringing them in and I had to pay my end by looking at them. He had them ready, inside his blazer and pulled them out, bent and curved at the edges.

We never thought he would dare bring in the pictures, but there they were, those glossy-coated snap-shots. The first one showed a raven-haired woman in nothing but red high heels sucking a vast cock. There was a lot of pubic hair and the scene took place in front of some heavy dull-coloured curtains. Flashlight bounced off the edges of lacquered furniture. It was a dining room: the kind of room that children go in and out of. The picture was vulgar, but the debasement of desire was fascinating. This was what adults did. They got on their knees in front of each other and begged. This was what being a grown-up meant. This is what they got up to when the children were not around. It would never be possible to think of one's parents or of Mr and Mrs Marshall in the same way.

There were other pictures too, fuck-shots from various angles, but one or two were enough and within minutes the cabal of boys scattered.

The pictures turned the school family upside down. Adult authority was based on the maturity and balance they possessed, which was contaminated by contact with the disruptive world of children. But the pornography showed the other side of the screen was full of red and black dressed-up sex and we realised that adults only existed as adults in the moments they were with their children. It was confirmation that they were, in effect, our responsibility. Without us around, they might be utterly at the mercy of the horned goat.

I wondered at the medical relevance of this image. Having got over the initial shock, I wouldn't have minded taking a closer look, but the pictures were gone and I knew we were in trouble. One of the boys was going to get all soft about the thought of Mummy chewing on Daddy's pee-pee. It was just a matter of time.

And so it proved. A boy, name unknown, got up early and went to find Mrs Marshall and her vat of bubbling porridge. He was upset by the pictures of the cock. Before long, Mr Marshall had a list of all the boys who saw these pictures and we were hauled in, one after the other, to be questioned. It was impossible to deny that I had seen the images. But beyond that, there was confusion as to how to proceed. Could we be punished for looking at something? Were we victims? The head of the school family was confused and passed the buck to the genetic family.

My father would have to deal with me. I was worried about that but what I was really frightened of was that my misdemeanour would cause one of those awful four-act domestic dramas that my parents went in for. The angry, probably drunk father, the swearing and shouting: the protective mother crouched in front of her children: the paternal hangover and subsequent weekend in which they would shut themselves into the bedroom, talking and doing whatever. Actually, I now had a much better idea of what they did. There would be days of exhausting emotion, all my fault, and at the end of it, Dad would seem weaker and my mother stronger than before and, of course, that wasn't any good either. If he lost the battle, he would just resent me.

At the end of term, my father came to collect me, wearing his RAF uniform, driving up from Buckinghamshire on the usual tube of Pro Plus and packet of fags. He was called into the headmaster's office while I waited anxiously in the hallway, convinced I would be cuffed around the head. When my father came out he was subdued and soft. 'Come on, Willie,' he said. 'Let's go home.'

We drove in silence through the rain, back down the A1. I immediately hid at the bottom of the garden. I could see through the kitchen window that my parents were talking, not shouting at each other. Dad had a cup of tea; mum was poised over the sink. They were looking at me, peering, as if they were frightened.

'We hear you saw some nasty pictures,' my father said when I came back in. 'You all right about it?' I nodded. He hummed and looked relieved. 'Well, we won't say anything else about it then, will we?'

I had spared them. The sex thing would have been a nightmare to talk about. Their desire for each other had made fools of them both.

Once I had seen sex, I could not pretend it did not exist. It was a vital factor in working out the problem of grown-up behaviour.

During the summer half-term of 1975, I stayed again at Bramble Carr. My eldest brother Nick was also there on and off. It was a puzzle where Nick went during the holidays, but even at fifteen he had a way of disappearing that was to be the pattern for his subsequent life.

Dorothy seemed especially weary. On the Saturday came Egton Bridge Conservative Fete for which she spent two days baking cakes. She was too tired to go to the fete so George took me. I couldn't find a loo and wet my pants. George couldn't smell anything because of the pipe. I confessed to Dorothy who smiled and washed my shorts for me.

The next day Dorothy seemed at a loss and encouraged me to walk over to Rowantree Farm, which I had not visited for a while. Brenda Tindall asked me to stay for tea, but we had barely sat down when the phone rang. Brenda answered it.

'Willie,' she said, quiet and anxious. 'It's your brother.'

'You'd better come back,' said Nick. 'Something's happened. Uncle Robert's going to take you back to Barnard Castle.'

I remember it as being night when I walked back to Bramble Carr, but it was the afternoon, just overcast with clouds. Dorothy was lying on the small sofa in the dining room next to the kitchen. She was making strange bleating and wailing sounds. Her stout legs stuck stiffly out from under her skirt and her body twitched like a beetle. I couldn't get close enough to see much of her face. Over her stood George and Uncle Robert and the doctor, Bob Robinson. The room stank of shit.

'Ah, Willie,' said George, gentle in his shock. 'Your grandmother had a stroke. You had better go and wait upstairs.'

An ambulance took Dorothy away. Afterwards Robert drove me back to school. He had an old estate car, a Rambler, full of empty Coke bottles and fag butts.

'What will you do when the ashtray is full?' I asked.

'Buy a new car,' he said. He lit another Benson and Hedges and stared out of the window. In those days he had a shaggy head of hair and a small unkempt beard, looking sweet and wild. It occurred to me that Dorothy was Robert's mother. What must he be feeling? He didn't seem upset. He chewed his gum, smoked another fag, and cracked a few jokes. At school he gave me a pa on the head and a couple of pound notes. The head ster confirmed the details of what had happened and too the money from me. Thereafter, no one mentioned my gran '- mother's stroke.

I felt convinced that Dorothy would be better in time for the autumn term when I started at the Main School. What would I do otherwise? Life without George and Dorothy would not be possible. It would be inconvenient of her not to get better so that she could come and sit beside me in the school chapel, vibrating to the music.

I was only to see my grandmother two or maybe three times more. She made some sort of recovery and lost a lot of weight. It changed her character; I remember her standing in her kitchen with a grim look on her thinning face, aggressively shaking a packet of All Bran. There were no more cakes or butter; the pantry was empty and her clothes hung loose. Her eyes sparkled with meanness and she was prone to sarcasm. The anger that had been buried inside her bulk came to the surface and I could not love her as I had before. I felt desperate regret at this.

She died in the summer of 1976, a year after the first stroke, suffering a massive secondary that put her into a coma from which she never emerged; she was just sixty-four. I only found out she had died by accident. I called Bramble Carr and discovered that the wrong people were there. Uncle Robert answered the phone and passed it over to my mother. Mum! What on earth was she doing in Yorkshire? My parents hardly ever came north. I guessed the reason before she spoke.

Robert dealt with the death in his usual droll way. Looking down his mother's body, he said: 'Well Ma, at least you died thin.' He phoned around looking for a funeral director. She had often shopped at the Co-op in Castleton and had a dividend card, so Robert rang them. 'Is that the Co-op?' he asked. 'I hear you give good value for money.'

It was so hot that summer that there was a rush to get her buried and I couldn't go to the funeral. When George died, ten years later, I missed his funeral too. I had not seen much of him in those last years.

After Dorothy's first stroke it became impossible for me and my brothers to stay at Bramble Carr for exeats and half-terms. We went instead to my great-aunt, Tart, Dorothy's sister, who had a little cottage at Thornton Le Moor. I was also farmed out to friends from school. Sometimes they were real friends, sometimes boys with whom I was encouraged by my parents to cultivate prag-matic relationships. I felt embarrassed, and obligated. I could not wait for the day when I would not be dependent on anyone.

Thirty-five years later, my mother talked to me about the background to Dorothy's first stroke. I knew Dorothy had struggled with her weight and health, but I had not realised the extent of her personal frustration or her rage with George. I suppose I had felt it: that heaviness she emanated must have been a kind of depression.

'She said to me after the stroke that she was going to make George suffer,' my mother told me. 'She said, "Now I'm going to make George suffer." Why, I don't know. But she said it to me. "I'm going to make him suffer." And she did.'

At the time we talked, Mum was working all hours. She was always busy with dogs and chickens, a big house and garden and family. Moreover, my father, formerly so active, had not been well. He had a hip replaced and perversely became less mobile. His neediness had exacerbated the problems in their fifty-year relationship, from which the desire had long faded. To top it all, Mum had just bought a cow which she was keeping at a farm up the road and was spending a lot of time training. She put it on a rope and led it round in circles for hours on end.

I did think that there was something odd about the way my mother was speaking. She liked to talk, intelligently and widely, but now she could not end conversations. She repeated phrases and seemed stuck in a verbal loop. Her eyes looked bright but unfocussed.

Two days after our conversation, Mum was brushing the mud off one of her dogs when she had a stroke. Dad's hip problems meant that he rarely went out, so he heard her fall and got the ambulance.

I saw her in the hospital that night. Mum was flattened, crushed to two dimensions, red and bloated. Inside the immobile, strawberry-coloured face, were her eyes, peering out of her wrecked body as if asking if it was safe to emerge. She could move her left hand well enough to take hold of my hand and held on to it for the next two days.

Her stroke was of the severest kind, but the second night after it she was sitting up and painstakingly drawing pictures of trees and animals, knitting her mind and body back together. She indicated that she wanted to see something; she wanted me to bring her something. Did she want to see my father? Dad? No! She drew a cow; she wanted me to bring a photograph of her cow.

7

MODERN LOVE

I was upset to learn about Dorothy's comment after her first stroke that she was 'going to make George suffer'. Even if I accepted that she had been unhappy, why did she say such a hateful thing? What had George done that deserved punishment? He had not given her the stroke: she was fat, lazy and smoked.

I wondered if there was a simple explanation, something that would explain her implication that she had been seriously wronged. Sexual jealousy was the obvious motive, and I was intrigued to learn that George had probably had an affair several years before they moved to Bramble Carr.

The evidence did not point to anything especially passionate. My aunt Rose remembers that as a toddler she was taken by George to a village outside Guisborough where they went into a nice house and met a nice woman and there were cakes and sandwiches. The woman and George seemed to know each other well and Rose surmised that she had been taken somewhere that was to be seen only by children who were too young to ask questions. That was it, so far as any witnesses went.

It seems unlikely that this tea-and-cakes arrangement so enraged Dorothy that she wanted to use her last days making George suffer. Perhaps there were other loves. Women liked George; he kept his lean looks and in his sixties he could still manage a handstand on the edge of the kitchen table, using only his arms to raise himself from the floor. Along with the looks and strength was his melancholy, which was intriguing if you weren't married to it. If George was philandering, he made a good job of hiding any twinkle of pleasure.

Dorothy herself had a romantic weakness. She was fond of clergymen and quite open about the boyfriends she had before she met George. I was told by my mother that Dorothy also became infatuated with a dashing swindler whose family owned a pub in Guisborough, and gave him her savings to invest. She lost the money and her sister Tart bailed her out so that George never knew.

Sooner or later, all partners have to deal with over-familiarity. Estrangement is often nothing to do with what happens in the bedroom, though it can be everything if that is all there is to the relationship. My grandparents' marriage had been about more than sex; they had been companions. They had talked, and then George stopped. Soon after Dorothy moved to Bramble Carr, she met Brenda Tindall. 'George is so bloody boring!' she told Brenda. 'He won't talk to me!'

This, I think, was the source of her anger. She could comfort her body with food but it was her mind that needed stimulation. All her fascination with life which George had once shared was left without an outlet. He put her into a prison of silence. They had argued about the existence of God and the relevance of Alban Berg and whether Pablo Casals was the true interpreter of Bach's cello suites. Now they managed a joke about people with names like Winterbottom.

They had become their parents. George was a version of his silent father, Dorothy her suffering mother. It was impossible to say precisely how and when the young couple had been replaced by these older models. The process was uniquely human, subtle and unintentional.

Over the year between Dorothy's first and second strokes there must have been some bad evenings for both of them at Bramble Carr. How claustrophobic that setting must then have seemed; how much like a trap into which life had driven them both.

The marriage had been nothing like that at the beginning. For its day, it was a bold relationship. They were an intellectually modern couple, who tolerated and even admired each other's beliefs. They had strongly differing views about politics and religion. She voted Tory, he voted Liberal. She liked High Anglicanism and might even have converted to Roman Catholicism were it not for the Methodist influence in her roots. George, whose parents had been solid Church of England, approached faith with the analytical care that he used in so many situations, whether dealing with a family crisis or helping me with my maths: 'Now then,' he would say, 'let us assess the situation, review the facts and consider what we can say is or is not the case.' He could not know for certain, and so he could not believe. Yet he did try. In the 1960s, he took to reading Teilhard de Chardin, the Jesuit palaeon tologist whose work, though suppressed by the Vatican, was then reaching the public domain. De Chardin attempted a synthesis of science and Christianity which placed human evolution at the centre of a universal design. Mankind would advance to a technological point at which it must assume the work of the creator God in order to achieve its destined union with the Divine. Sex would be eliminated from reproduction. De Chardin's work is poetic, visionary, passionate, a vivid and honest portrayal of an individual soul searching for a way in which it can be faithful to both loves, a frantic spiritual adulterer. George tried, sighed and went back to his *Times* crossword and pipe. It could not be said to be the case.

George and Dorothy argued loudly in those early days. There was chemistry in their relationship, an attraction between elements that had strong affinities and equally strong disparities. As opposites they coexisted; they admired each other. But as the conventional married couple, they stopped arguing about important things. The debate became about George's refusal to fix the door.

If Dorothy was embittered by George's withdrawal, what in turn had caused him to fall silent? In later life, he confessed to friends that he felt he had failed professionally, though there does not seem to be anything obviously disappointing to his career. He studied chemistry at Sheffield, specialised in glass production, and after marrying Dorothy, found a job working for Boam's, a family firm based at Leziate, outside King's Lynn in Norfolk.

Boam's had been quarrying for fine-grained glass sand at the village of Leziate since the mid nineteenth century. During the Second World War, Leziate became an important asset as high-quality silica was essential for clear glass required by arms manufacturers. There was a lot of research, much of it secret, into the purification of sand. George was involved in the development of aircraft canopies and bomb sights.

His work also led to a long involvement with the research committee of the Society of Glass Technology, analysing sands from new British sources. He saved the Society's correspondence in a box file. Much of its work was devoted to the search for some definitive process of glass purification, which, from the largely irritable letters exchanged between many eminent chemists, seems to have been regarded as an attempt by a few fusty types to exert control over a process that had many ways and means.

In the box file are a couple of poignant curiosities. There is some excited correspondence relating to the possible patenting of a process, and a certificate of service for the Home Guard. The former was something that Dorothy sometimes alluded to, the context being that George, though clever, was naïve and had let his ideas be stolen. The certificate records that: 'In the years when our country was in mortal danger George Leslie Brooks gave generously of his time and powers to make himself ready for her defence by force of arms and with his life if need be.' George kept guns under his bed and used to shoot rabbits and pheasants out of the window. He told his sons that he would have liked to have had a crack at the RAF but he was on the reserved list because of his work. Uncle Bill remembers George getting tearful about the fact that he did nothing in the war except take a shot or two at a rabbit. He would have been in his thirties anyway during the war, and too old for flying.

In Norfolk, George and Dorothy rented Holt House, just behind the quarries at Leziate, a rambling hotch-potch of ancient and modern, half-timber, half-brick, a ghostly house without electricity, lit by candlelight and paraffin lamps to which clouds of huge hawk moths thronged on summer nights. It was rural and quiet with more horses than motor cars. During the war, the night sky thrummed with the sound of aircraft leaving Norfolk to bomb Germany. Far away, at the edges of vision, the world sometimes caught fire.

For miles, the fields were open and empty, rough pasture and thick clusters of oaks. Leziate itself was wrapped in forest. The soil was a curious red, like rust, with silver deposits of sand leaching to the surface all over the place. It was very well drained, and drier still from the winds to which it was exposed.

In Norfolk, the first four of their five children were born: Muriel, Mary, Rose and William. Dorothy found it hard being a mother to so many children and often sent them to stay with relations in Doncaster or Worksop. Tart also helped look after them and there was generally another friend or two in the house. Dorothy hated being alone and never spent a night by herself.

What was Dorothy doing having so many children when what she had wanted to do was play the piano? The babies exhausted her. She kept her figure after the first, almost after the second, but then began eating. Was it genetic compulsion, or was it that she thought she must produce a son for her husband, something her mother had not managed to do for Willie Ellis? It was as if she had set about to contrive a situation that she would be unhappy with, a situation that would provide her with a reason for her dissatisfaction.

The children undoubtedly influenced George's decision to move jobs. He needed better pay and security. Dorothy egged him on; she wanted to get out of Norfolk. In January 1947, he went up to Welwyn Garden City for an interview with ICI. They paid him £1.80 for his travel expenses, reimbursed by cheque, and a month later he had a letter confirming his appointment as a plant manager in the plastics division, working from Billingham on Teesside. The salary was £700 a year for a standard forty-three-hour week. The contract had a clause that forbade any outside research or publication. He resigned immediately from the Society of Glass Technology and became a company man.

A visitor to Teesside today will have no idea of the splendour that was Imperial Chemical Industries in its full post-war glory. An orange smog still hangs over both banks of the Tees, a warm blanket of aromatic cloud, but only the skeleton of the chemical industry remains, a few clusters of factories that have passed through dozens of owners. In between are hundreds of acres of undecided dereliction, towers and chimneys and warehouses with a lean sense of purpose in their design, buildings that once possessed a robotic life, now snuffed out. Rusted pipes go here and there. Fencing closes off rubble. It is like a mouth with the teeth pulled.

There is nothing left of ICI itself, though some of the factories it built are still active. The iron bridge still spans the east end of the Tees at Middlesbrough: this was the artery that once connected ICI's plastics and ammonia divisions north of the Tees with the new chemical city the company created on the south side of the estuary at Wilton, just sixty years ago. The chemical giant came and went so fast.

ICI was founded in 1926 through the merger of Brunner Mond, Nobel Explosives, United Alkali Company and the British Dyestuffs Corporation. Famously, the merger was planned between Sir Harry McGowan (of Nobel) and Sir Alfred Mond (of Brunner Mond) on a voyage from New York to Southampton on board the *Aquitania*.

Both Nobel and Brunner Mond were vast concerns, the former manufacturing explosives, the latter heavy chemicals, but independently neither was a match for the Germany chemicals monster IG Farben or the American du Pont. Post-war, business was sluggish in the explosives trade: Nobel wanted to diversify into chemicals. Brunner Mond was also casting around for new products: it had recently bought an ammonia plant at Billingham from the British government and had big plans for fertiliser production.

In those first years, trade tariffs guaranteed ICI its Imperial market and in 1927 ICI made a pre-tax profit of £4.5 million. But, from its inception, the company was a chaotic web of operating groups in a state of perpetual reorganisation. Production overlapped and competed. Eventually it was slimmed down into seven production divisions, but it was still the case that nobody really knew exactly what ICI made, apart from everything. At one point it owned Sunbeam motorcycles.

During the Second World war ICI built and ran some twenty-five factories for the government. It produced explosives, ammonia, chlorine, light alloys, polythene, Perspex, agrochemicals, pharmaceuticals and poison gas. ICI even played a role in the development of the atomic bomb before work moved to the USA. After the war, when cheap oil became available for the production of artificial fibres, ICI entered its smoggy, stinking, golden age, in which it spewed out new products, making polythene, Perspex and PVC available to the public.

This plastics revolution required massive quantities of chemicals and a purpose-built plant. Wilton, on the south side of the Tees, seemed perfect. It had good transport, access to cheap fuel, and easy effluent disposal into the poor old river. Wilton Works opened on 14 September 1949, two years after George first went north to work for ICI. It cost £20 million and was a new kind of factory, a chemical factory of the age of oil. There were no brick buildings with tall chimneys smoking away. No rattle and crackle of coal; no soot. This was a vast stainless steel chemistry set.

By 1951, ICI employed 131,000 personnel. The plants at Billingham and Wilton became futuristic cities of writhing metal pipes, great distillation vats and steel chimneys glittering under the sun, covered by their own weather system of steam and vapour, their breezes of aromatic ammonia, chlorine, alcohol, sulphur and plastic blowing far inland. At night, the industrial world of Teesside was brilliant with lights and flaring gas, the energy supplied by the North Tees Power Station, which ICI had taken over. ICI was a state unto itself. At Billingham, ICI quietly operated a small General Atomics TRIGA Mark I nuclear reactor.

ICI was a decent employer. It offered employees

discounted shares, had the same working hours for the factory and office staff and recognised the unions. In time there was a profit-share scheme, a cultural and educational programme with a Billingham Folklore Festival and a sports complex. There was a football team: Billingham Synthonia, the only football team in Britain to be named after a synthetic product – synthetic ammonia. The company offered George and Dorothy financial security. It also defined them.

If they felt unsure about where they belonged in the world, these clever, culturally curious children of the working class, here was a completely new world that seemed classless. It was a corporate machine. Once you handed yourself over to it, there was not only material security, but also democracy. Forget where you came from or how you spoke: it was the corporation that would decide how high or low you moved, to what use they could put you among their vast range of products. This was where new things were made, substances that were not in themselves natural, new kinds of glass and fibre. Perhaps, in this extraordinary mix of intellect and industry, some brave new class of people was emerging, a technical meritocracy.

George had enjoyed the experimental side of glass production, but that was old stuff. The future was going to be plastic, not glass. He disappeared into the labyrinth, moving from one production plant to another, from one chimney to another, inhaling the sweet whiff of alcohol. Above him went his own little plume of St Bruno.

Dorothy would not have to be alone in that huge Norfolk house, with the moths banging on the window. They moved to a rented house in Middlesbrough, where the children choked and coughed and developed rashes under a pall of fumes. Above them was a massive trailing windsock of orange smog that pilots could use for navigation purposes, hundreds of miles off.

One of those pilots would be my father.

8

SWEETHEARTS

Dorothy owed a great deal to her sister, Tart, for the help she gave her with the children. In her discreet, intelligent way, Tart was the secret strength within Dorothy's life, the childless sister who made it possible for Dorothy to function as a mother. She is ubiquitous in the family pictures, holding the babies as much as Dorothy. Her real name was Muriel but she was known as Tart because that was the word that came out of my mother's mouth when, as an infant, she tried to pronounce 'aunt'.

Not only did she come to stay with Dorothy but she later took in Robert and Bill when Dorothy felt she could not cope. Tart loved the boys to bits. She even said Bill could live with her, if Dorothy thought she had a bit too much on her plate. Dorothy got huffy and said Tart had turned Bill into a Mary Annie, a bit of a pansy. Tart was a confidante to both Dorothy and George and apparently knew all about George's affair as well as Dorothy's involvement with the swindler from Guisborough.

My siblings and I adored Tart. In the early 1970s, she still owned a sweetshop and general store in Northallerton.

She had two stinky old Yorkshire terriers called Bonnie and Della and was married to an odd bloke called Ron, who as children we knew little about except that he had been a crane driver and had suffered a bang on the head which made him a bit slow. He sat out the back talking to the parrot. We liked the sweetshop. Ching! Ching! went the bell, and another half-pound of ham or a quarter of sherbet lemons was dispensed before Tart returned to the back room to smoke another Embassy Gold.

In contrast to Dorothy's more romantic expectations, Tart lived a life that was an object lesson in making the best of things. She had no illusions: the daily round was hard. She sold consolation in quarter-pound bags of boiled sugar, sweets that were probably made in Doncaster, just a few miles from where she had been born. She loved to laugh: she would laugh until the tears ran down her face.

By the time I had moved over to the main school and needed somewhere to go at half-terms, Tart had retired from the sweetshop to Rose Cottage at Thornton le Moor. Ron had died, but the dogs Bonnie and Della lived on and on; either they were immortal or had been replaced with identical specimens. I can still remember the fluid skinny bodies and bad breath of the minute, bronze-haired creatures.

Rose Cottage was a pretty, cosy place. It had a neatly tended front-garden path, lined with roses and gladioli. The front door opened directly into the small sitting room; out the back an extension permitted a kitchen and a second bedroom upstairs. Behind the house was a long garden; Tart grew her own vegetables and had, my mother remembers, a green finger when it came to shrubs and plants. In a paddock was a caravan that provided overspill accommodation.

Tart kept a coal fire burning most of the year, creating a drowsy fug thickened by cigarette smoke, and the cottage was given a heartbeat by a grandfather clock that stood in the back shadows of the sitting room. The clock had come from her parents, she said; it had an eight-day German chime mechanism, with a long, lazy tick-tock and the hours sounded with a loud rattle and boing. She had a huge affection for the clock, as if it was a companion. A surviving receipt shows that she paid £28.75 to have it serviced in 1980, a lot of money thirty-odd years ago.

Next to the fire Tart had her colour television, a big one for those days, and she sat in front of this watching *World of Sport* and smoking her little Embassy Gold fags, chucking the butts on the fire. She loved the wrestling. For fans this was the era of Kendo Nagasaki, Giant Haystacks and Big Daddy (real name Shirley Crabtree: his 64-inch chest was dressed in a leotard said to have been fashioned by his wife Eunice from their chintz sofa). The sight of vast men in aggressive ballet costumes sitting on top of each other had a comic menace. Did they really hurt each other or was it all a pantomime? Tart watched with serious-minded incredulity. If you sat with her, through the dark of a winter's afternoon, she would stand up every hour or so, chuck another cigarette butt on the fire and say: 'Shall we have a creme egg then?' There was a stock of Cadbury's Creme Eggs in the drawer of a side table. In those days, the eggs were generally not on sale until Easter time. But of course, she had been in the trade and knew where to get them.

Tick-pause-tock went the big clock in the dark corner. Tick-pause-tock. When there was no wrestling she watched the snooker. As at Bramble Carr, there was no central heating in Rose Cottage. Instead, there was a storage heater and in winter, if it was very cold, an electric bar fire was put in the spare bedroom. 'Don't use it unless you have to,' she would say. 'Just the one bar.'

As my grandparents had seemed to me to be products of the moors, so I imagined Tart had been born among toffees and bon-bons and gobstoppers, with her apron on, her hair up, and wearing her big glasses. After she left her shop pinny behind, Tart always dressed in a plaid skirt and cardigan. Winter or summer, Yorkshire or Australia, she wore a sensible skirt and a cardigan. She was small and stood straight, light on her feet, heels together and toes out. She had nice legs; several people said that to me about Tart.

At school in Doncaster Tart had shown herself to be exceptionally bright so her marriage to Ron perplexed my grandparents. Ron seemed all right to us kids, the way he spoke to the parrot, but Dorothy found him uncouth. Even liberal-minded George thought him a bit thick for someone as clever as Tart. Ron spent much of his time sitting out the back of the shop in his brown overalls; he was too big for them and his upper body seemed about to burst out. He was a burly, slow-speaking, big-featured Yorkshireman, who liked to whistle and hum and sing and make silly voices He was spivvily handsome, with slicked hair and a big jaw. His knees had gone and then his back, so he couldn't do any work except help out Tart.

When Dorothy and Tart's mother, Annie Louisa was widowed, she went to live over the sweetshop. 'Louie' was put out by her new circumstances. She sat by the window dressed all in black, and refused to come downstairs when the shop was open. To get attention she banged on the floor with her stick. Ron had a bit of banter going with

Louie. He called her 'closet' which was the rudest sort of word a properly brought up working-class lad like him could use. 'It's the bloody closet,' he would say when she banged on the floor. He would take her lunch on a tray and they would have a stand-off; they were fond of each other in a sneaky way.

Sometimes Ron seemed temperamentally incontinent, immature, and confused. He lost his temper with an old woman who came into the shop, asked for a single slice of ham and complained when he cut it too thick. He called her a closet too. Tart gave him a telling-off afterwards. She had to do that sometimes, especially when he got drunk. He was always sorry and sad at himself, but soon he'd be back to humming again.

Bill and Mary knew Ron couldn't take his beer and used to drag him to the pub to sow trouble. A couple of beers and Ron would be singing 'I'd liiike ter get yer on a slooow boat ter China' and doing the high-hat fills, boom-chinga boom-chinga boom-chinga bang on the rhythm and then Bill would get Ron another pint and suggest to him that his sister-in-law, Dorothy, who affected such disapproval of the raw, sixty-something lad, was secretly nursing a passion for his rough animal side and longing for him to plant a kiss on her smackers. 'It seems to me, Ron,' Bill would say, in his newly acquired Aussie drawl, 'that's she's up fer it.'

'D'yer think soo?' Ron would say, with excitement. Back at the shop, he would advance on Dorothy, bearing down on her boozily, saying, 'C'mon now Dorothy, give yer old uncle Ron a kiss,' while she squealed with displeasure and Bill and Mary and Tart laughed until they cried.

Perhaps it was because Tart had spent so much time looking after Dorothy that she had no choice in the companion stakes. Maybe there were other reasons she chose Ron.

It was love, I discovered: a love that was in its way more enduring than my grandparents' love. Tart did not marry until she was gone forty. In a small leather photo frame, tucked behind an old passport picture of her, is a yellowing news cutting announcing the engagement of Ronald Barnett Kirkland, youngest son of W. Kirkland and the late Mrs Kirkland, and Muriel, youngest daughter of Mr and Mrs J. W. Ellis. There is a picture of her wedding, with Ron looking huge and cheerfully Kray-like next to his composed and happy bride, both of them middle-aged but young with excitement. Ron towers over Tart; she was even smaller than I remember. When I think about it, Ron was rather like one of those burly yet dainty wrestlers that she watched, hour after hour; she liked a big bloke.

Ron's family, the Kirklands, were also from South Yorkshire. His brother, Fred, was the postmaster at Braithwell, between Doncaster and Worksop. Their father, William Kirkland, had been postman at the small village of Maltby, just down the road. William Kirkland had been a special postman. Among Tart's papers, I found a flat case containing an Imperial Service Medal, and a crumbling newspaper cutting. 'Postman cycles 180,000 miles – Farther Than from Earth to Moon!' William Kirkland had received the medal on his retirement in 1937, after thirty-five years on his round.

In a brown-tinged photograph, the moon-bicycling postman poses in his uniform for a final photograph. Behind him the brick terraces are bleached out by the sun.

He holds his bicycle as proudly and tenderly as any lancer might his horse; the canvas bag on the handlebars is empty. He knows his round is delivered, his job done.

Ron volunteered in 1940, and was a leading aircraftsman in the RAF. There are pictures of him in uniform during the war, his dark features concentrated around the bridge of his nose, giving him a cross-eyed look, amiable but lost. It was during his stint in the RAF that he got the bang on the head. He was on his bicycle late at night when he was struck by a lorry and thrown into a ditch where he lay unconscious and undiscovered until the next day. Fortunately, it was very cold, which probably inhibited blood flow and saved him from the worst brain damage, but he was left with no sense of smell or taste.

What struck me as odd about the pictures Tart had of Ron was the sentiment they contained. My mother identi-fied a snap of two teenagers – him with a big quiff, her with a big pale face and frizzy hair – as being Ron and Tart. Yes; there they were, together as kids. How odd! They had known each other since childhood and from his doting gaze he had been in love with her then. As in their wedding photographs, they looked as if they fitted. Then why did Tart have to stand smiling at so many other weddings before she had her own?

The postman's marriage certificate gave an answer. In 1907 William Kirkland had married Mary Ellen Cable, the twenty-eight year old daughter of Fred Cable, a brewer's porter. This was the Fred Cable who I knew was Dorothy's maternal grandfather. Ron's mother was there-fore Dorothy's aunt, so Tart had married her first cousin. Ron was a relation of mine by blood as well as marriage. First cousin marriage is not illegal, though it has carried a social stigma for its incestuous overtones and the possibility that the union will increase the chances of genetic problems. It was not the done thing, and the fact that quiet old Tart married her first cousin, and possibly had a long love affair with him prior, was never mentioned. Ron was just the funny bloke with the Brylcreemed hair.

At some point, long after he had banged his head, they seem to have decided that there was no longer any obstacle to the pair of them being together. They were just sweethearts, far too old to have children. He adored her. She was often impatient with him, but appreciated that she was the centre of his life; if he was like a child then that too filled a gap for her. It had been a lopsided love, but it worked.

Tart's relationship was one of low expectations, in contrast to Dorothy's marriage, and also to that of their mother. Louie had been deeply romantic. When she died she left behind a small notebook, from which the covers had long since fallen. Into this she had copied recipes for gingerbread pudding, rice meringues, lemon buns and cough medicine made with treacle and peppermint. But at the end of it she had written a poem:

Do you know you have asked for the costliest thing
Ever made by the hand of God
A woman's heart, & a woman's mind
And a woman's wonderful love

Do you know you have asked for a priceless thing
As a child might ask for a toy
Demanding what others have died to win
With the reckless dash of a boy

I am fair & young, but the rose will fade
From my soft young cheeks one day
Will you love me then in the falling leaves
As you did in the month of May?

Willie Ellis had not appreciated the gift of Louie's heart.
Tart did not lay herself open to such disappointment. I often
look at the pictures of her with a half-pint glass in her hand
and a Yorkshire terrier on her knee, her shrewd and gentle
face half-hidden behind huge spectacles. There were things
she could have told me about the nature of enduring romance.

If only I had known a bit more back then. If I had
known, for instance, that the crane driver who spoke to
the parrot was not some interloper in the cultured world
of my grandparents; that the bumbling leading aircraftsman
was me, just as the dashing RAF officer who married my
mother was me. I would have been more affectionate to
Ron and later, his existence would have reassured me that
there was nothing wrong about my feeling that I was out
of place, that I belonged not only at a public school and
Oxford, but equally on a building site or out the back of
a shop.

These things have gathered significance with my need
to find some affinity with the past and understand my
occasional unease about the present. To Dorothy, contact
with Ron had the reverse effect. She felt uncomfortable
because he was a reminder of where she had come from,
the Doncaster monkey that was always at her back,
mocking her progress.

In another picture, Tart is leaning against the front door
of her sweetshop. It is a Victorian doorway, with an overhanging porch with finials and a fanlight, supported by

slender Doric pillars and topped with winged beasts. She has her hands in the pockets of her pink working dress: the sweetshop front is blue. Beneath the window of the shop is a pavement advertisement for Wall's Dairy Ice Cream. The window is filled with jars of boiled sweets. A sign tells us 'Senior Service Satisfy'. She looks contented; this is home. In the bottom of a box of Tart's papers, along with William Kirkland's Imperial Service Medal, I found a Stratton powder compact. It could not have been opened for thirty years. I recognised it as Tart's; it smelled, just as she did, like a sweetshop.

9

POSSESSIONS

All through life we collect possessions we wish we could dispose of. We believe our hearts have become too divided by our attachment to things, to books and pictures and furniture, as well as to houses and even relationships that seem to be worn out. From time to time it seems that if only one could get rid of this junk we would rediscover our essential selves.

It takes a disaster to see how necessary the familiar can be. My mother's stroke was serious enough to kill her; instead she recovered with remarkable speed. She rebuilt herself from shards of her life, using the drawing book she kept by her bedside, forcing herself to scrawl pictures of her familiar world, to construct letters and then words, showing the same delight a toddler has at fitting the right word to the right picture. She later said that when she was lying in her crushed and bloated state, she had an out-of-body experience. Looking down on herself, she could see which neural networks were damaged and how she would have to re-route things. At first she could only use her left hand to form letters on the page; eventually, to the astonishment of the doctors, feeling began to return to her right side. She wrote down the names of her children, her friends, her dogs.

When my father came to visit he sat by the side of her bed trying to say the right thing and failing. He would tell her to hurry back home as he had just bought some fresh mussels. Mussels! As if she cared. They had to have a new car and he brought a grey Skoda which she said looked like a hearse. She made him sell it and buy a blue car.

Mum felt that one of the reasons for her stroke was the growing anger she had felt with Dad. It had been a stormy marriage from which the passion had gone, leaving them without much to say to each other. Like Dorothy, my mother needed to talk. She needed to talk about feelings and Dad could not. Mum's frustration had become centred on this inarticulate man. She was convinced that if she could crack him open things would be salvageable. He was happy to talk about the contents of the newspaper but when it came to anything more personal, he sat at the kitchen table, folded his arms and said nothing. When he was young that glowering exterior had been part of his attraction. Now it made him look infantile.

In some ways, Mum's stroke spawned hope. Mum's absence had animated Dad. He had enjoyed taking control of the household environment, so we all wondered if perhaps she would ease off her domestic routine and concentrate on doing some of the things that gave her pleasure. She might start drawing again – she did wonderfully flowing yet precise life drawings – or she might travel a bit.

The thought of being looked after by her husband horrified my mother. She required her routine to help her recovery; she needed not only familiar things, but the familiar feeling of control. With that the familiar conflicts quickly returned; the arguments over who had said what to whom thirty years ago, whether or not it had been a badger or a fox they had spotted on the road the other night. It was inevitable that if Dad repeated an opinion he had heard Mum express, then she would leap to assert the contrary. He, in turn, ruffled her poise with calculated coarseness, shuffling down the pub, drinking too much.

My mother resented my father. She admitted it. She had tried to love him, and she never said, as her mother had done, that she was going to make her husband suffer; but the year that followed her own stroke was one of profound suffering for both my parents, when they seemed to sit at either end of a see-saw of their communal existence. How the hell had things ended up in this situation again, just as with George and Dorothy?

My mother had regained much of her speech and was moving well when I took her to visit Danby. It was early summer; the weather was fine and warm and she walked easily up Danby Rigg, sometimes stopping to feel the ground with her shoes, casting around, as if the directing stream of her consciousness had been momentarily lost. Up by Fatty Betty she sat on a stone and told me where it had all started going wrong, which was pretty near the beginning, fifty years before.

She had met my father when she was training to be a nurse at Darlington. There was a dance into which Dad and a few other young RAF pilot officers had blagged their way. After a few minutes, he suggested they go and sit in his car, where he said he had a crate of beer. She refused and thought she wouldn't see the good-looking but arrogant young man again. At the hospital the next day she was told that a young man called Tim Cohu had come looking for her and had left her a bag of apples.

'Always food,' she said. 'Even then.' She wasn't sure that she liked him. She was attracted to him, but there was something about him that made her feel uncomfortable – something inchoate that she feared. But she was won over by the glamour of the officers' mess, the bowing and scraping of the batman, and the uniforms. The Battle of Britain was a recent memory and the RAF boys were still the nation's heroes. My father's parents made a fuss of her, especially my grandfather, Air Vice Marshal John Le Mesurier Cohu, CBE. John Cohu flattered Mum and Dorothy. He liked beautiful women.

Dad drove a Jaguar, and he flew Lightnings. He really could fly brilliantly. He came roaring up the Tees valley in a Lightning, right over the house at Hutton, a supersonic streak of silver, adored by my uncles Robert and Bill. Even now, around Danby, old men – just boys in those days – can remember my father and the excitement of knowing that he flew Lightnings. Designed to intercept long-range Russian bombers, the Lightning had stacked twin engines; it was the only British-built fighter capable of Mach-2 performance and it had a phenomenal rate of climb. Lightning pilots could stand the plane on its tail and rocket skywards. Was there any more potent male image than that?

My father persisted. He proposed to Mum in the car and she accepted. He eventually got round to giving her a ring that had been his grandmother's, though it later proved to be worthless. They got engaged and Dad went off to Aden to bomb camels for eleven months. They saw each other for a few days again before the wedding and had a brief honeymoon in Devon before Dad was posted abroad again, this time to Kenya, with the understanding that Mum would join him when he had sorted out a house.

By this stage, Mum had got over the initial excitement of the marriage and had decided she'd made a mistake. She did not like feeling that she was owned by anyone. She was pleased Dad had gone away and she went back to her parents at Hutton Lowcross outside Guisborough. Months passed; she stopped thinking about Dad and resumed her love affair with horses. She started riding again, accompanying the aged local squire Sir Edward Pease on long leisurely hacks across the moors. Sir Edward, who had been badly gassed in the First World War, in which he had won the Military Cross, had a double first in Oriental Studies from Cambridge. He was a gentle man who suffered from shellshock, and spent long hours asleep on the floor of his study. He rode in full white bee-keeping attire with a veil. Mum preferred his restrained company to that of my father. She felt sure that by some miracle she would be spared a resumption of a relationship that she now feared.

But there was no miracle, and she could never articulate the magnitude of her error. George, who loved her dearly and could see that she was troubled, told her that it was all right if she had made a mistake. But Dorothy was less understanding. If Mum tried to express her doubts, Dorothy would round on her. 'You're married now. Get on with it,' she said. 'Enough of that silliness. Do you hear? No silliness.'

Mum was sent for. She was packed on a train to London,

bussed to Wiltshire and marshalled on to a turboprop Bristol Britannia, where wives and children were packed like cattle and flown to Nairobi. When they stopped to refuel, Mum stepped out into a gasping hot night, pitch black and stinking; her feet splashed in puddles of sewage. In Nairobi, Dad had not sorted out a house. He took her to a motel for the night. The next morning, he drove her outside town to the edge of the bush, pulled over and pointed down a dusty side road. 'Walk down there,' he said, 'and you'll come to the house of a girl called Liz. She'll look after you. About half a mile. Go on, out you get.'

In a wretched, uncertain state, Mum climbed out. He would surely not drive off? He could not! But he did. The dust settled and she saw she was surrounded by curious black faces. In an instant her confidence drained from her. She couldn't remember what Tim had said, which direction he had pointed in. Surely not that way, into the bush and the dust? Panicked, she set off in the opposite direction and walked for hours around Nairobi, horribly lost. An elderly, genteel Belgian eventually rescued her, took her to a hotel bar and made her have a drink. She spilled out her story; the Belgian could not understand her husband's behaviour. How could her husband leave her wandering around alone? This was Africa.

When Tim finally rented a house, he chose a remote bungalow outside Nairobi which he liked for the game-shooting – zebras and antelope. It was the aftermath of the Mau Mau Uprising: the house boys were restless and Mum was frightened to be left alone there. Dad continued to behave as he wished. He drank; he went out late at night and sometimes didn't return. He expected to be looked after and flung his shoes down to be cleaned. She could not challenge him. She knew she had made a mistake, but she was by now not only married but pregnant. Quite how it had all happened, she could not say, but quite contrary to her intentions, she had been caught.

Why had she said yes? It had been a moorland romance in which they had both been swept off their feet by looks and sheer drama, by the attraction of their shining silhouettes in this smouldering setting. Up on the barren moors, the ambiguous, fanciful elements of a personal story take on an almost unquestionable authority: how can you turn away from the significance of the occasion? It seems fated. My marriage would also be a moorland romance, a relationship that was cemented on a fog-bound walk over Danby Rigg, when around us the world had disappeared until it seemed that the only thing that was of any importance was the other. Romance is an uneasy gift, though life is deathly without it.

My parents were married at Guisborough Priory, with my father in dress uniform and my mother in a white dress and veil. There is a wedding album we all still look at, amazed at the perfection shown in the pictures. When Uncle Bill visits he always wants to see it. He still feels as he felt then, almost in tears at the loveliness of the occasion. They were such an implausibly handsome couple. My father with his sulky, bad-boy Continental looks and a softness around the eyes, like Montgomery Clift, but darker and more yielding. My mother was classically elegant with a wonderful nose and a delightful light in her face; like Audrey Hepburn, but stronger. There is one picture of them staring into each other's eyes outside the church and smiling. They look as if they could eat each other.

George and Dorothy's wedding photograph is also unintentionally revealing, though in a different way. He is dressed in a single-breasted suit, with a striped tie and white carnation in his buttonhole; she is in dark velvet. He looks excited and a little embarrassed at all the fuss. She leans her hip into him, her right arm clutching his left arm. Down her front spills a bouquet of white roses and ivy. They appear comfortable with each other. There are two copies of the photograph. On the back of one copy, some mysterious hand has written, 'The day of mistakes.' My mother and her sisters think that it was probably Uncle Robert who wrote this. It would make sense; if they had never married, he would never have been.

There is some writing on the back of the second copy and there is no doubt about the author. It is a shopping list, in Dorothy's handwriting:

1 Kitty Kat
3 carrots
3 cooking apples
1 Ryvita
1 dozen eggs
1 lb ham

10

EVOLUTION

George and Dorothy did not stay long in Middlesbrough before moving to the cleaner air of Guisborough, where they bought a modern semi on quiet residential Gill Street. Guisborough, a wild and pretty market town, was being transformed by the industrial forces on Teesside but it was still neighbourly. The children went to Northgate Primary school round the corner. There was a doctor nearby – very useful for Dorothy – and a fish-and-chip shop, to which the children were sent to buy ginger ale for their mother. Every morning, Bob the milkman would do his rounds of the Guisborough streets with a cart drawn by a massive Cleveland Bay.

They needed more space though, and in 1952 George commissioned the house at Hutton Lowcross on the southern edge of town, where an old mining community called Hutton Village was becoming popular with commuters from Teesside. They called the new home Holt House, after the place in Norfolk.

A larger house was needed not only because the children were growing up but also because their number had swelled. At the age of forty, Dorothy became pregnant with Robert. It was an unintended pregnancy and a difficult birth. The baby weighed ten pounds. Dorothy, overweight and unfit, had to spend a long time in a private hospital. Everybody knew that Robert was, in a sense, an accident; which did not mean he was unloved. Once he was there, Dorothy cared desperately and was distraught when the infant nearly died of pneumonia.

He was a gentle, affectionate and sensitive child, but anxious. At Hutton, he had a friend down the road called Malcolm East, a boy of about the same age whose father also worked for ICI. When they were six or seven, Malcolm and Robert ran away one night and hid in a garage in the centre of the village. At about 11 o'clock, they heard the noise of adults looking for them; the trudging steps, worried exchanges and their names called. Malcolm switched on his torch and saw a small smile creep over Robert's face as he heard himself being looked for. He knew he was missed and he liked it.

In his thirties, when he had followed his brother Bill to Australia and the black dog had got him well and truly cornered, Robert would go on and on to Bill and Mary about his feeling that he had not been wanted. So far as they could remember, Robert had been treated kindly. If that was how an unwanted child was treated then none of them were wanted. Dorothy was twenty-nine when she married. She had children later than was usual for her time. Naturally, this made things more complicated for her; she was often tired.

Perhaps Robert knew from birth he had not been planned: perhaps babies do learn, even in those first few months of life in the womb, whether they are wanted or not. Dorothy must have sighed a lot as she dragged her child-swollen body round.

When George built Holt House, Hutton Village was scarcely developed. The core of it was some thirty small cottages with communal washhouses and pigsties, arranged in three terraces on the edge of rising moorland, with a beck running down the middle.

The village lay at the end of a road that ran up from Hutton Gate station. The road first went gently uphill past meadows, past the brooding bulk of Hutton Hall and through the dense shade of overhanging trees, then climbed more steeply to the foot of Hutton and Guisborough moors. In a sheltered cup, where the roots of the moorland flowed together, two small spurs off the road encircled a green that formed the heart of the village. Beyond the village the road became a rough track that ran up the moorside to Highcliff Farm. The moorside was then open and treeless, though it was being planted up by the Forestry Commission and is now thickly wooded. From the mid 1950s, many new houses, and a good few ugly bungalows, would be built along the village roads, spreading back towards Guisborough.

Ironstone had been found here in the mid nineteenth century, then jet. The moorside was scarred with pit entrances and blood-red spoil heaps where shale was burned in clamps to expose the jet. This was a mining village and the sense of a no-nonsense, working-class community prevailed at Hutton well into the 1950s. The terraced houses were rented out to foresters, estate workers, and steel workers many of who went on to work at ICI.

There was a village church, known as the Mission, with

a tall fluted spire, and down the road was a pretty school with high gables. There was no pub, because the sober design of life here was dictated by the Pease family who were Quakers.

The Peases had made money from wool, mining, shipping, banking and the railways. They created modern Middlesbrough, buying up what was then farm land by the Tees, partly as a transit port for their coal, partly as an investment. They encouraged the first foundries to come and shepherded them through their early years. By the late nineteenth century the banks of the Tees were blazing with furnaces and the Peases were filthy rich.

Quakers were remarkable businessmen whose position as social outsiders seemed to free them to dare where others only dreamed. In many cases, Quaker businesses returned to their workers some of the wealth they produced, the model villages provided by the chocolate makers Cadbury being the best-known example. The miners' terraces at Hutton were not in the same league but nor were they squalid hovels. Pease money paid for the running of the local school, but the local railway station was at first only for the family's private use.

The fortunes of the Pease family waxed and waned. The family bank, J. & J.W. Pease, went under in 1902, after Sir Joseph Whitwell Pease's niece sued him for mismanagement of her inheritance: she won half a million – some £40 million in today's money, but nearly ten times that if you consider the sum as a portion of the national GDP. The feud ruined several of the family. Sir Joseph had to sell his art collection and died the next year. The private train station subsequently opened to the public.

By the time my grandparents moved to Hutton the

family's glory days were long past. Sir Edward Pease, 3rd Baronet, had left Hutton Hall – an imposing but gloomy Gothic revival by Alfred Waterhouse who also designed Strangeways Prison – for nearby Pinchinthorpe House, a much built-upon farm. Hutton Hall remained empty for long periods and was let at one point to members of the Plymouth Brethren, a red-haired family. These were serious non-conformists. Passers-by could hear a mix of screams and singing coming from the house. One of their sons hanged himself. None of the Brooks children enjoyed walking past the Hall at night.

George's new Holt House was nothing like the rambling Holt House in Norfolk. That had been rented; they owned the new Holt House and it represented a distinct social advance on their part. There was a decent kitchen and an adjoining dining room and a drawing room. Being a modern woman, Dorothy was a kitchen person: vicars and tradesmen, neighbours, teachers and musicians all sat in the kitchen and talked with the children present. When Annie Louisa visited from Doncaster, she sat by herself in the dining room.

'Why don't you come in here, Mother?' asked Tart, through the connecting serving hatch. (Tart was there, as ever, looking after Dorothy.)

'I'm not talking in the kitchen,' replied Louie. 'The kitchen is for servants.'

In this new world, the masters were also servants. Some, of course, were more likely to be one than the other and kitchen chat had a sly way of not making things any more democratic. Tart did more than her fair share. The arrival of the family conversation, with adults and children all having a foot under the table, must have seemed indecent to those like Louie. If you had done your time as a wife and mother, and struggled to keep up appearances, to be put in the situation where your life might be idly joked about by your juniors; how impertinent!

The miners' cottages and the village's association with the Pease family were reminders of a time when everybody knew their place in life. Things were no longer so clear-cut. Most of this was down to the new wealth on Teesside, where the chemical industries offered the chance of swift promotion from the ranks. Former manual workers who found themselves part of the up-and-coming classes could not easily abandon their traditional enmities. They sniffed suspiciously around my grandparents, trying to work out what kind of mongrels they were. They smelled of Doncaster and Worksop, of soot and corn, but from their house floated the sound of a piano.

Malcolm East, Robert's little friend, came from a different sort of family. Malcolm's father was from Redcar and had done his time working on the factory floor. He was now a senior engineer at ICI and part of the merit-ocracy, but still had a sense of us-and-them. He told Malcolm that the Brooks family were social climbers 'who think they're too good for the rest of us'. Malcolm repeated this to Robert, who laughed and said, 'You listen to your father too much'. Malcolm agreed with this. He did listen to his father, who was a regular, forceful male. Robert, on the other hand, rarely listened to George, possibly because George never said much to his sons.

Whatever complications the adults experienced with this process of social evolution, Hutton was a good place to be a child. Malcolm and Robert spent their days playing pirates around a copse that they called Treasure Island, sailing to and fro across a meadow and shooting flaming arrows made from bulrushes. Rose liked to go and play in the woods with a box of matches and one day set the hillside above Hutton on fire. She had never liked woods anyway: too spooky and dark and best got rid of. They played in the diggings the miners had left, which had been enhanced by trenches and foxholes created during the war when the Army had come to Hutton to train for D-Day. A short walk uphill and you were on the open moors, without restrictions. In those days George used to go for fifteen- or twenty-mile walks across the moors, sometimes taking his elder daughters. For holidays, he drove the family the short distance to Baysdale, one of the smallest and most isolated of the dales, which opens in the moors like an underground world, a long deep scoop of green among the purple heather, with one steep road into it from the north and three or four houses. It had once been the site of a small Cistercian priory, home to twelve nuns and a prioress, with a reputation for scandalous wildness.

Baysdale was not far from Teesside, but it belonged already to a distant past and its inconveniences seemed charming, in summer at least. The Brooks children stayed at Baysdale Farm, where there was no electricity, only candlelight, slept under huge down quilts, and spent their days damming the beck while George walked the moors and Dorothy sat cooling her feet in the water.

Hutton Village stood at a boundary between the mapped world and the wild places. The road that ran up through the village was gated where it began its steep ascent towards Highcliff Farm. Beyond that gate, not just the landscape but the people changed too, from industrial workers to foresters and farmers whose work was part of them, men made partly of wood and water and earth – men like Eric Hayes, the lithe, quick young man who had come from Halifax to work as a rabbit-catcher for the Forestry Commission and had stayed on to plant trees. He was thought to have an eye on one of the Brooks daughters, but he eventually married a Florey girl from up the road and took her off to live in a caravan in the woods. The boys liked Eric. He had a touch of the pirate.

The other way, back down towards Guisborough, was full of ghosts that spilled out of the shadows around Hutton Hall. Passing by the old gardens on a summer evening, children could smell the sweet spiced scent of mock orange blossom spilling from the neglected shrubberies. In the shady woods around the house and up the course of the beck grew Himalayan Balsam, the tall, pink-flowered Victorian garden favourite that is now a ubiquitous weed. The seed pods were an irresistible attraction; when ripe they needed only the slightest touch and they would explode, shooting the seeds a considerable distance, while the remains of the pod curled up on itself.

Children went to the cosy primary school and attended the Mission, a damp place where Dorothy sometimes played the piano. One family in the village, the Wilsons, had a television set, and invited the village children in to watch *Children's Hour* with Billy Bunter and Muffin the Mule. Up the road from Holt House, Mrs Gull ran a shop out the back of her house, selling household basics and sweets for the children. They crowded round when the van delivered the sweets. Most of them brought Rowntree's Fruit Gums, which could be made to last: twenty minutes a sweet was good going.

The murmur of local gossip rarely intruded on the children's lives. Mrs Gull was not a widow, but her husband was said to have 'gone away'. An eighteen-year-old girl fell pregnant and gave birth down the loo. The finger was pointed in turn at every young man in the village, but the father turned out to be a fifty-year-old former Army major.

Despite the way the country was slowly opening up in terms of class, some familiar dilemmas resurfaced. In their own ways, Mu, Mary and Rose were facing a repetition of the frustrations that had blighted Dorothy's life; there was no obvious place in the world for clever girls to use their cleverness. What use was it to prize high cultural values when they did not personally advance you and made you impatient with the traditional roles of drudgery that were on offer? You were being educated into a state of total unsuitability. Further down the family, my uncle Bill was also undecided as to whether it was desirable to climb the greasy social pole, and began plotting his own revolution.

From childhood, Bill had a latent temper. Later, booze worked on him like black magic, changing him from an easy-going, amusing charmer into an argumentative nightmare. There were tell-tale signs that the transformation was imminent: a change of pallor to pink, a ripe protuberance of the bottom lip and a jiggling knee – the knee was a real gauge. You watched that knee carefully.

Now in his sixties, Bill has mellowed considerably. I know few people who have endured such tragedy in their lives. First, he lost his brother Robert; eight years on, his eldest son Joe, who had followed Bill into the merchant navy, was killed in an accident on board a ship; a few years later, his adopted son Matthew committed suicide after a long battle against drink and drugs. Each death affected Bill deeply and changed him, but not in a predictable fashion. The accumulative effect of such tragedies might be expected to crush a man. Bill has acquired a paradoxical serenity. He used to be arrogantly charismatic, with a pugilistic swagger. Now he intrigues and attracts people with his intangible hurt: they sense that he has suffered and may know something that could help them.

In the course of writing this book I talked with Bill a lot. At first I was curious to hear about the childhood he had in Yorkshire and grateful for any light he could shed on my grandparents' relationship and how that might have influenced Robert. In the end, I became as interested in Bill as in these other subjects: they were in a sense, the downward curve of the story. But Bill had survived so much and it was impossible after talking with him not to feel more optimistic about life. He led the upward curve of my thoughts. At the time, with my mother's illness, my father's death and my own collapsing marriage I needed reassurance, preferably from a father, but mine had just died, and was not much of a talker anyway. In Bill I found, accidentally, a father figure who I fancied had also become the man Robert might have been had his life not gone awry: a mixture of rough and tender, sharp-witted and honest about his failings. It was that last quality that really struck me. Bill questioned himself and his own responsibility for past events without abject apology and with the determination to live better. He had not reacted to catastrophe by becoming introverted. He was if anything more open, curious about life and other people. I knew that in the past he had often been surrounded by a cloud of domestic chaos, and I would not have liked to have been his son. For all his good intentions, his boys were almost too close to him and perhaps grew up too fast under his super-masculine influence. But the value of a man is not just in success or failure, but in how he can interpret and pass on his experiences, which Bill did for me. Even the sound of someone describing their distant disasters can be a help. It was good for me to know that one day, I too would be talking about things in the past tense.

Bill still looks at the whisky bottle wistfully, as if it were a lover he fancies a last fling with. When he came to stay with me in Lincoln, where I was living after my marriage ended, he was impressed to find in one of the kitchen cupboards, otherwise empty except for children's breakfast cereal, an unopened bottle of whisky. 'Now, look at that,' he said. 'You are evidently a man of considerable self-control.' That made me feel better; it also made me laugh. I hadn't touched the drink because I knew that it would lead to a hole of self-pity. Bill and I, though similar in many ways, were different in that. He got angry when he was drunk: I felt sorry for myself.

The sober version of Bill's temper was a simmering rage, which I think gave him a huge propulsive energy when he was young. Rage is an ambivalent force. It stands in for a whole lot of other qualities you feel you lack, like courage or persistence or brains. When all else fails, you can call on the rage. It is a generic form of emotion, unbranded and flexible. It is like an adjustable spanner. It never quite fits and in the end it burrs everything. But it can do a job. Rage sometimes kept Bill going when nothing else would. It was rage that sent him flying from Hutton and landed him on the other side of the world.

As a boy he loved his parents, and appreciated the benefits of their liberal values, but he could not help also feeling rage about what he thought was the imbalance in their relationship. Bill liked to read adventure stories about burly, masculine men who fought wars and climbed mountains. The characteristic of such a man was that he was not pushed around and Bill disliked the way that George was, in Bill's view, dominated by Dorothy.

Bill did not want to be an academic like George. He wanted to be a sailor, or better still a pilot like my father. Bill adored my father, the film star in his dark blue uniform with his Rothmans between his lips, rolling up in his Jag or tearing over the village in that silver Lightning: how glamorous the RAF seemed, how virile!

There was a problem in the dynamics of the Brooks' household. The place of the man was more complex than before. No longer was the wage-earner master when teamed with his intellectual equal. Dorothy was top dog and George disappeared behind his pipe smoke.

Boys need to fight their fathers, not feel sorry for them. The self-respect of both father and son depends on a kind of honourable conflict. I don't think I ever had that with my own father, and my relationship with him was all bits and pieces until things came together when I was in my thirties.

The whacking stopped when I was seventeen and I told him that if he hit me I would smack him back. He looked surprised and retreated quietly. In my twenties, I found myself drawn to clever drunks as father figures. They were charming, depressive, cruel and pitiable. Were they some sort of amalgamation of my parents? Did they reflect aspects of Old Hay? Or Dorothy? I lurched this way and that in trying to find some role model. I simply never got to grips with Dad when I was growing up. I didn't see him that much and when I did, we rarely spoke. If one of the boys needed to request something of Dad, we had first to approach my mother who assumed the position of negotiator. She was acting in our interests, she thought. The arrangement saved a few rows, but it did not permit much honesty. Mum took the flak from Dad, but in return she had all our love. Hidden behind her, my father loomed like a distant mountain top, seeming more mysterious and perhaps bigger than he was.

Bill felt he had a weak father, and so took up the battle with Dorothy on George's behalf. He acquiesced to her cultural instincts, studied the violin and listened as she beat out the rhythm of a piece of music on the table with a knife and asked 'What is this?'

But he hated the inner heaviness she had, that passive frustration. He wanted to goad her: she wanted everything to be 'peaceful and agreeable', as she put it. It seemed to him that peaceful agreeableness and liberal discussion permitted a regime of constant small-scale regret and discontent about which nobody did anything. He'd listen to her complaints and think, Edmund Hillary has climbed Everest and you're sitting here sighing. I'm getting away. Then he'd stomp out and get on the bus and hear the local women gossiping in their Yorkshire accent and feel revolted by the cosiness of it all.

'Oh, shut up, William,' Dorothy would say. 'Don't be so silly, William.'

He argued with Dorothy, and when he could not win he manipulated her. For a while he went to the primary school at nearby Nunthorpe and it was the job of Rose, the youngest sister, to put him on the bus.

One day, when he was five, he didn't fancy the trip and pretended to be dead, lying down at the bus stop motionless. Rose got into a panic and when she managed to resurrect him she took him home, where she told Dorothy, 'William's dying.' Dorothy was furious. She sent him to his room and told him he could have only bread and water all day.

He decided on a strategy of unremitting cheer. He took the slice of dry bread that Dorothy left him and rolled it into twelve little dough balls, setting them in a row. When his mother came up the stairs to see how the prisoner was faring, he greeted her, smiling bravely: 'I'm fine, Ma! Look! I've got my food here. I'm going to eat one now, and another later. See . . .' Dorothy began crying. He knew exactly what he was doing. He had the ability even at that age to add footnotes on his own behaviour, often highly critical, knowing that it wouldn't prevent him from doing the same later.

Later, Dorothy used to sigh when she heard George, back from work, playing a Beethoven sonata, especially when he hammered his way to the end of Opus 111. 'If he plays like that I shall run away,' she would grumble. 'You see, how can I ever play again when he plays like that?'

Bill would say: 'Well, at least he tries.'

'Don't you talk to me like that young man!'

She would whack Bill with a hairbrush or sting the

back of his legs with a bit of soaking mutton-cloth, or she would pinch him, saying: 'I'm going to pinch you: I'm going to NIP you!'

Only once did George raise his hand against his elder son, and then it was on Dorothy's insistence when Bill had, despite persistent warnings, been running around the half-built walls of the new house opposite. George offered Bill a choice of loss of pocket money or six of the best. Bill had experienced many sixes at school without much noticing them, and reckoned he had a hard arse, so he opted for the latter. George used the flat of his large and hoary hand in a way that left Bill yelping and weeping and at the same time, full of admiration. If only George had been more assertive with Dorothy, Bill felt, and had used the flat of his hand on her bum. Instead, the house was full of women who all wanted things to be peaceful and agreeable.

England seemed miserable. Bill knew the world was changing. His father worked at the forefront of science; the new industries were creating wealth and elsewhere the shops were full of good things. At Hutton they seemed stuck in the past; even the newfangled coke boiler was, in Bill's opinion, bloody useless. It went out and had to be started up all over again in the evening; eventually warm water would circulate to the radiators but by morning the house would be freezing again.

He was cold and hungry. They were not poor; he never thought there was a particular lack of anything, or thought he was neglected, but he was so bloody hungry. The family watched each other to see who was getting more. The children craved sugar and fat. Dorothy would steal the cream off the milk and blame the blue-tits.

The grocer came in his van to take orders and sat in the kitchen, in his white coat, chatting to Dorothy and in between snippets of gossip, she would place an order for half a pound of flour and Bill, lurking by the table like a crocodile with disgruntled, greedy eyes, would say: 'Coca-Cola.'

'Be quiet, William! No Coca-Cola!'

'Coaco – coala,' the grocer would say, in his Yorkshire accent, with a snigger. 'Coacoa – coala!'

Sometimes the children were given threepence each to buy a packet of fruit gums from the grocer. The others made them last; Bill stuffed them all in his mouth, until the juice ran down his chin. In Nevil Shute's novels he read of the plenty in Australia which made him hungrier still. It wasn't just the food he longed for. It was the space, the infinity of Australia and the distance from Hutton.

He sat at the kitchen table with his father, building model aircraft, wishing he could grow wings and fly away.

11

NEW PRODUCTS

If George appeared to be dominated by his wife, the girls of the family wondered if she had any alternative, since he was so aggressively passive about everything. 'No' was his response to most requests from Dorothy. Would he discipline his sons? No. Would he talk to the teachers about the boys? No. Would he speak to the farmer who lunged amorously at my mother? No. Far from being liberal, it was as if George was applying a gruff version of his father's lack of attachment and shifting all responsibility for managing life on to his wife. He was domestically less demanding than his father, but had created a new range of issues for a wife to deal with – more difficult problems than ensuring that his collars were starched. If Dorothy seemed larger than she ought to have been, it was because George had no interest in being any bigger himself.

George seemed at a loss when dealing with the incongruities of human psychology. He was good at finessing the cracking of hydrocarbon bonds and stringing beads of molecules together, long chains of them that made up plastics, hanging a molecule of carbon or hydrogen here or there, but not much good at fathoming relationships. He did have a feeling for attachments that might be damaging, hence he was wary of my father, who was possibly a bad molecule. Success in chemical production depended upon the consistency. One bad molecule could spell anarchy.

At Billingham, George supervised the production of a range of ICI plastics products. There was Perspex, which had been used for Spitfire canopies and was just being released into the civilian market for use in lamps, cigarette boxes, bar fittings and cocktail cabinets. He also looked after Transpex, a variation on Perspex for optical lenses in cameras and projectors; Kallodent, for making dentures; Kallodentine, for fine denture finishes; Mouldrite synthetic resin adhesives for bonding wood in furniture manufacture; Nuron resin for contact pressure laminating; Welvic polyvinyl for cable coverings; and all kinds of Alkathene, which was the trade name under which ICI sold its polythene products. Out of the factories came a stream of new products, doing what nature could not do.

From time to time he led an experiment in hybridisation between the natural and the synthetic. When ICI produced a prototype decorative hard plastic that was enhanced by the addition of fish scales, George brought home several tea trays made from this new stuff; there was a crimson one and a white one and they had a deep lustre to them, shimmering with the scales trapped inside them as if there was a moving shoal in there. They were pretty but couldn't take heat and warped. It was unwise to mix worlds; things didn't turn out how you expected.

There was this ordered, logical side to George, yet he

was also a romantic, otherwise how could he have ever loved my grandmother? He longed for some sort of metaphysical experience. Again and again he had a dream that he told to my mother, a dream that he was flying, leaping from mountain peak to mountain peak and he would wake up happy and shouting 'Weee! Weee!' at the memory. Then there was the music; he was so impassioned by Beethoven that he had taught himself to play the piano: the imperfection of his technique never troubled him. It was the feeling he required.

With his children he settled on dependable, fixed relationships, reliable but not organic. It was hard for him to adjust his perspective as his children grew and changed. He treated them rather like products that had arrived fully formed and functional. He adored my mother and was fearful for her; he had a kind of companionship with Rose, whom he respected, but he got on best with Mary who seemed to share his intellectual detachment and his taste for the dry *mot juste*. It was Mary he took with him on his walking holidays to the Lake District. He was most comfortable where there was least emotional complication. With the boys, he was affectionate but hapless, at his best when they were very young and could share his enthusiasm for building model aircraft. His detachment was a reflection of his own insecurities; it was not that he did not feel, but that he feared feeling too much.

There was a general ambivalence in the family about expressing one's true feelings. This was reflected in the way the children talked. On the surface, everyone was highly articulate and had a way of speaking that was bookish and smacked of the King James Bible, or Malory's *Morte D'Arthur*. He smote his breast, there was a mighty to-do, then the skies did open, water came forth from the eye. The language mocked everyday tribulation; when real dilemmas emerged the children could find themselves unexpectedly short of the means to express themselves directly. They were trapped by bathos. Emotion, as their mother's life instructed them, had to be productively employed in art. That was where you expressed your inevitable personal tragedy. Without the frame of art, feelings were silliness.

At primary school, all the children were bright and happy but as they entered their teens, they became aggressively uncooperative. My mother went to Redcar Grammar for Girls. Each morning, she bicycled down to Hutton Gate, ostensibly to catch the train. Instead, she hid her bicycle in an old shed on the edge of the woods and walked west over the moors to Great Ayton, where she knew the family who ran the chemist's. She would hide there all day.

Across the road from where she was playing truant, her sister Rose was supposed to be attending the Friends School, a Quaker establishment that occupied the handsome Georgian buildings running the length of the village green. Rose had survived meningitis when she was an infant but it took a kidney and the core vision of one eye and knocked her back at school, so she had to be educated privately for a while. At the Friends School pupils were encouraged to stand up and talk if the spirit moved them, but were whacked when the spirit said the wrong things. Rose was instinctively independent; she hated the punishments and hated the miserable food and used her pocket money to play truant in Middlesbrough where she loitered around the sweetshops. It was typical of the family that despite its conversational closeness, not only did neither parent know their children were bunking off, but the sisters themselves did not talk about it.

My mother felt awkward in her teens. Her dreamy, fawn-like beauty attracted men; she was not flattered when various local farmers, whose horses she exercised, all began proposing further mutually beneficial arrangements. It was noticeable, from early on, that my mother was most comfortable in the company of older gentlemen who treated her with helpless gallantry. She liked animals more than people, dabbled with the idea of working on a farm but eventually went to Middlesbrough College of Art. Mum had – and still has – a special talent for drawing life figures, which her children all wish she would use more; she often promises that she will, then finds reasons not to. Her sisters had their talents: Mary played the violin and Rose had a musical ear, too; but in the end they all became nurses.

Dorothy did not push them directly into leaving home. Rather, her gravitational pull went into reverse and was now an energy directed at expelling her daughters from her orbit. She did not wish to be responsible for them. She would cajole and nag, looking sideways at her daughters, from under lowered lids, a haughty look. 'Now, my girl,' she would begin. 'What you need to do is . . .' At the same time, she fiddled and dabbled in their lives and relationships, sometimes with wilful destruction: her ideas about good partners for her children seemed at odds with her own emotional and intellectual requirements, as if she didn't want them have any more happiness than she had enjoyed. How perverse she was.

She also took to her bed, demanding her daughters help her out around the house, which had the effect of making them feel that if they did not escape they would end up looking after her full-time. Dorothy had always struggled with the practicalities of domestic life. Food was scarce at home not because George and Dorothy were poor, but because Dorothy hated shopping. There would be a roast at weekends and cottage pie afterwards and soups and something from the garden, but as the week went on, the food supply would diminish as the children grew bigger and hungrier with each passing day. Rose was upset about the food situation. There was no need for it. Dorothy did not seem to go without. Why was she, Rose, so much smaller than her sisters? Because Dorothy underfed her, of course.

'Nonsense, my girl!' returned her mother.

'Then my size shows I'm a marital lapse on your part,' retorted Rose, evading the hairbrush. Even today, you won't catch Rose going far without something to eat in her pockets, an apple or a few biscuits.

Dorothy's occasional home help was Annie Howard, an ageing woman who lived in the miners' terraces and used to be seen wandering around the village dressed in black, leading several cats on a piece of string. She smashed everything of value. When something went wrong, Annie would point upwards and say: 'I told you so. He'll be reaching out and tapping you on the shoulder.' The children thought that Dorothy kept Annie around to play the Fool to her Lear.

The girls knew they had to get out or be sucked into the general slackness of the household. It was the forceful rebuff of Dorothy's simmering discontent. Later in life, it always seemed to my mother that the moment she came to stay, Dorothy would take to her bed and demand she be looked after. Times had changed since Dorothy was a child but a girl's dilemma was much the same. They were new products with the same old problem. There wasn't the money to launch them independently. Where were they to go? Where did these independent-minded, bright girls belong in the new world?

Everybody needed nurses. You could travel if you were a nurse. You didn't have to worry about class distinctions either; all sorts of people went into nursing. As with the armed forces, nursing was one of the ways to cross boundaries. You also met men, lots of different men. That was how my mother met my father. In escaping from Dorothy, she ran into Tim.

The boys went into the merchant navy. Both had won places at Guisborough Grammar, where they refused to deploy their intelligence. Bill's report for 1961, when he was fifteen, puts him somewhere near the bottom of form IV. His English was all right – 'an interested pupil with a genuine feeling for words (which alas he cannot always spell)' – but everything else ranges from 'not very satisfactory' through 'very poor indeed' to 'shocking for a boy with his ability'. Scripture wasn't too bad. Bill liked a lively debate.

Bill wanted to go into the Royal Navy. He needed two A-levels to get to RN College, but he was doing so badly he was told he wouldn't get a sixth-form place. Dorothy wept. 'George, do something,' she cried. 'No,' he replied, once more, from the kitchen table. It was obvious that Bill was bright, but he fancied himself as too clever to try. He was in the end offered a sixth-form place, but he had by then decided to leave school at sixteen and go into the merchant navy.

The maritime academy at Southampton was a paramilitary institution attended by boys from all backgrounds. Bill noticed the posh voices as soon as he arrived, the lazy lah-di-daahs of Etonians, the ease and grace and presumption, which put him in a tizzy of excitement and loathing. On one level, he had a ferocious sense of identity, based around his stubbornness and his innate confidence, or arrogance, or both, but he could not shake off the feeling of not knowing where he came from, for which he blamed his mother's social pretensions. She, that ball-busting woman, had denied her children their working-class heritage.

Bill could have run off and become a builder if he really felt the urge, but he wanted to go upwards as well as downwards. He knew it was wrong that a bloke should have to crawl for acceptance. So he hated these posh fellows even as he longed to be liked by them. His voice was an immediate problem: his Yorkshire accent, with its long flat 'o's and short sharp 'a's was cruelly imitated. When he had to give parade-ground commands, like 'stand fast' he became confused as to whether he should use short vowels or long ones, and stammered into silence. The other cadets laughed at him. He raged back. He was sensitive and impressionable, dogmatic and fierce, verbally dexterous and bitter, quick to confront, yet soft as butter, lazy yet sometimes striving to a fault. He was a mystery to himself.

He was always in trouble at college, just as he had been at school. He could do the stuff if he tried, but he needed a clear head. Why did he have these rages, and this habit of falling in love with the shadows of other men? He even had problems with basic mechanical movements. He sometimes couldn't tell his left from his right when parade-ground commands were shouted at him. If he thought about it, in that crucial split second, the certainty that there was a difference between left and right would disappear, and he would wonder how and why they were distinguished and the injustice of such an arbitrary distinction and then any difference between them would vanish and his decision as to whether he turned left or right would be completely random.

At his passing-out parade, he was fallen out as the bugler, because he was such a pathetic parade-ground performer. He had in fact taken up the bugle as a means to avoid the parade-ground torment, since the bugler played while the other marched. He was good on the bugle, and played the 'Last Post' with real feeling. Nonetheless at the conclusion of the passing-out parade he had to rejoin the column. With his parents watching from the stands, he became confused at a left-turn command, stepped boldly off, thinking he was now at the head of the column and then realised he was going in the opposite direction to the others, a boy apart. He had to about-turn then make yard-long strides to catch up. His officers seethed. In the stands, Dorothy wept again, this time with laughter.

Bill had at least sorted out his Yorkshire accent. He was sure that once he had a uniform and the right voice and worked amongst people for whom deference to uniform and voice was natural, then he would be fine. When he turned up for his first ship he was not quite seventeen. He stood at the bottom of the gangplank, spick-and-span in his new uniform, with his huge new trunk. At the top of the plank the quartermaster was about his business. No one noticed Bill. He walked up the gang-plank: the quartermaster glanced up and down and did not salute. Bill thought about taking issue, then considered the size and ugliness of the man and thought better. Instead, he asked him where he should go.

The quartermaster jerked his thumb vaguely in the direction of a door: 'Yer feckin' go in there, yer feckin' go this way, 'n that way, feck off down some steps and yer'll feckin' find it.'

'Thank you. May I have some help with my trunk?'

'Ya what? If you want that feckin' thing aboard you'll have to feckin' carry it yourself.'

Below decks, in the cadet quarters, he found several dirty lads with a half-drunk crate of beer.

'Now then, look: it's arrived,' one of them said. 'It's arrived: it's feckin' arrived,' they all jeered. None of what he thought would be important mattered: not the uniform, nor the accent. What mattered were practical skills and he possessed none. They wanted mechanics and carpenters and he could play the violin. The crew picked on him mercilessly. His ears burned red with shame. The other thing that mattered was a willingness to use your fists. That he had, but he took a few beatings along the way, though nothing he feels he didn't deserve.

When I talk to my mother, uncle and aunts about the past, I know there are gaps in what they say. They have conflicting versions of what life was like and occasionally indiscreet memories of each other, nothing serious, but the general nature of their childhood memory is much the same. They share a collective impression of a largely content family at the kitchen table and none of their individual struggles alters that sympathetic picture, though it is possible for the mind to be in two places at once on the matter of one's parents, simultaneously critical and accepting.

About Robert, they share a collective fug, as if his death had made the previous stuff of his life irrelevant. After childhood he went off the radar. They were adults in a world that expected them to grow up fast, while he was still at home. Robert trailed behind the others. Like them he was happy at primary school. He started well at the Grammar but then went off the rails. Like his brother, he had a sharp way with words and got into a lot of fights. He was inconsistent, inattentive and his conduct was 'very poor indeed'. Only in scripture did he attract any praise, as if he was synchronising himself with his elder brother. By the time he was fifteen he came to life only when there was an argument to be had, especially in history where he expounded some 'outrageous' ideas. Robert always did have theories about the authorities. One, I remember, was that 'they' had a secret euthanasia programme to get rid of all the old people.

To Malcolm East, he remained a star. He got Malcolm through his English O-level, telling him what to write in the course of their many walks back up to Hutton from Guisborough. Brooksy: Malcolm called him Brooksy. Like his brother, Robert knew he was going to get out of Hutton: he was going to be a sea captain and what use was academic achievement to an adventurer? George never remonstrated with him. The dominant male was his brother; he adored Bill and, for lack of other male guidance, he dogged Bill's footsteps. It was by no means a straightforward relationship. Bill loved him, of course, but when he was young Bill needed to feel the whip in his hand. Even now, Bill's bottom lip juts and his face shuts down when he thinks about those childhood years. He wonders if he was cruel. He thinks he was a bully at school. A few years ago he joined Friends Reunited and had a stinging response from someone who had been at Guisborough with him, asking was he still the same little shit that he had been then and accusing Bill of ruining his life. He was quite shaken. 'I couldn't even remember him,' he says.

Bill says he does not believe that there are ultimate psychological causes for the blackness that devours people like Robert. It must be a disease. Christ, he tried so hard with Robert: they all did. But even so, he cannot help wondering if he played a part in the way things turned out. Could he have treated Robert too harshly when they were kids? Did that make a difference? What should he have done? A suicide does that. If you begin to wonder, there is no stopping: you go back into the shadows, snatching at events that are half-recollected, refining the past in the knowledge of what has happened, mixing history with supposition until you start falling into the dark yourself. You are asking questions of an absence and end up hearing echoes.

It was tough for Bill, too, to find that in the absence of a strong enough father, he had wound up responsible for his brother. Robert trailed him everywhere, like his shadow. That burly, confident exterior Robert had when I was a child was in part an imitation of the brother he admired.

Robert followed Bill to naval college and went to work for the Port Line who sent him back to university to study navigation; then he was off on container ships. He came and went in our lives, changing size and shape. At one moment he was a slender, dapper, uniformed figure, the next a ballooning slob with a beard, then a long-haired hippy in cheesecloth. He drove a series of awful cars that belched fumes and turned up at the front door of my parents' house, having driven hundreds of miles to see my mother and have a meal cooked by her. Children got smothered in a bear hug. You wouldn't see him for another year or so. He'd say something like: 'I had a girlfriend but there was a hole in the bottom of my car and she got stones blown up her fanny,' then he'd be gone again.

He made himself bigger than he was in many ways. On the ships he tried to be rougher than everyone. He drank more and he fought more. But it wasn't him. Somehow, it just didn't suit him but he could not permit himself to be anything else.

Malcolm East, whose life took quite a different turn, had stayed in Guisborough and went into dry cleaning. One summer's day in the 1970s, Brooksy turned up out of the blue. He was off to see his parents in Danby and dragged Malcolm to the Seven Stars: it was ten to three, just ten minutes to last orders in those days. Robert ordered eight pints for himself and three for Malcolm. Half an hour later, they were back out on the street, their heads spinning. Eight pints in half an hour.

He was taking drugs too. He had begun smoking grass in the early 1970s. Then there was that business with the dope up at Bramble Carr. There were a lot of new chemical products on the market, not all of them made by ICI. At

Southampton, where he had been sent to study navigation, he dabbled in LSD. He told Rose he had horrible memories of his trips. Bodies and worms. While I was at the prep school and stayed at Bramble Carr by myself, I used to listen to those cassettes of seventies hippy music Robert had left lying around, puzzling at the anxious English melancholy of Pink Floyd, at imagined vistas of a landscape smothered with soft rain. Robert was living the inner life of the music – a paranoid vivacity.

12

HAND-IN-HAND

My mother still thinks that behind my grandmother's decision that she must live at Bramble Carr Cottage was the conviction that she would one day move from there to the big house across the drive. I can see this is possible, though it was an absurd idea. A large house would have been impractical even if my grandparents could have afforded it. Perhaps it was not the reality of the big house that mattered, but what it represented.

Music had been the important thing for Dorothy, a thing of the spirit. Desire for an attractive home was a consolation, a bit like those Ryvitas she ate with all the butter on them. It was art, but fossilised.

There was no chance that they would ever go across the drive so there was in the purchase of the more modest Bramble Carr Cottage a sense of possessing her dilemma: there was the big house, but always out of reach, just as her musical ambitions would never be fulfilled.

My mother shared Dorothy's romantic interest in houses but her siblings did not care where they lived provided it served its purpose. They looked at an old house and, like

George, they saw tedious physical obligation where my mother saw affectionate duty. For them, a home was not to do with walls. A home was the place in which you felt accepted. Walls could easily become a prison.

My mother took up Dorothy's baton on the house front. The first house my parents owned was an old Georgian farmhouse in Lincolnshire, pretty but just thirteen foot wide. It used to bounce up and down when lorries went past. In 1990, they bought the wreck of a Victorian rectory up on the edge of the Wolds.

Ten years of hard work and they turned it into a charming house with a lush garden; they got on much better when they had this kind of project to do together. The place was filled with glass and prints and pictures and bits of antique furniture collected down the years. It became the family hub, where Mum seemed forever to be providing shelter and food to sons and daughters on the way into or out of marriage while my father, who had retired from the RAF, pushed his grandchildren on the swings hanging from the cherry tree on the lawn. He had good relationships with his grandchildren. I suspect that his distance from them made it easier for him to show his affection without fear that they posed a threat to his status. It was noticeable, however, that after a few days with a full house, he would begin to ask guests, 'So, what are your plans?' If he was snappy with small children, they had a way of dealing with him that quite wrong-footed him: they simply did not take him seriously.

I went one better than my parents, buying with my future wife a vast old Victorian rectory up the road from them. I loved the place, but knew at the time that I was buying it for all the wrong reasons – because my parents admired it and my future wife wanted it.

The house turned into a ten-year project: it provided me with the opportunity to show some aptitude for the practical skills that my ancestors had possessed – and I learned a great deal about the composition of lime mortar – but it also put me in my place. I pretended to be master, but I ended up a gardener and builder like so many long-dead family members. I was still, all these generations on, not working for myself. When the strain began to tell, I tried to be happy, but happiness is often the accidental consequence of making the most honest decisions and these are not always the obvious or easiest ones.

My wife and I had three lovely children, all of whom fortunately possessed a sense of humour. The relationship lasted nearly thirteen years, and there were long periods when we got on well, but we lacked some central, shared idea of how to live. We never fitted, though we swapped roles, first one then the other trying to take charge. We were like a pair of chickens with one head between them. If we ever did fix on some shared destination in life, we would disagree utterly about how to get there and at what speed. She thought I went too slowly: I thought she went in circles.

At one point, when we were attempting a fresh start, we went to look at a ruined, mud-swamped farm on the edge of Castleton Rigg, within sight of Danby churchyard. It had been owned by the same family for four hundred years; the last family member, a woman in her sixties, had been removed by the social services when she was discovered living in a caravan in the yard, knee-deep in refuse. We tried several times to buy the place but were thwarted. It would not have changed things in the long term anyway.

In trying to move back to Danby I was remembering the farming lives I had admired as a child; those hard-working couples who went hand-in-hand through life, facing down the problems together and holding on to their corner of the earth. I fancied that if we could make some version of the magical Rowantree Farm I had known as a child, things would be better. But I was never going to be like lean and indestructible Bob Tindall, and my wife was emphatically not Brenda.

The last couple of years of my marriage were mostly silent, as it was the only alternative to shouting. There is a thread of silence that has run through my family's rela-tionships, a way that men in particular have dealt with situations they cannot change. There are different kinds of silences, some despairing, some hostile. At times my silences were both, but they sounded indistinguishable.

The worst family silence on record was between Dorothy's grandfather, Fred Cable and his wife Martha. She had scandalously left a respectable farming family to marry a brewer's porter, and after having four daughters, she bolted, leaving Fred to bring up the girls. Martha worked as a gentlewoman's companion before returning to Fred in Yorkshire when she was old and ill. He shut her in the upstairs bedroom and, so the story goes, never spoke to her again. She lived a good few years in that room.

It seemed to me that Danby might be an ideal place to move to, because of its accommodating social mosaic of old families and incomers. Looking down from Danby Rigg, you would think that the area was solely about farming. In reality it has been unusually open and transient for a moorland community, because there was freehold land for sale here – which was not often the case in the moors, where most land had remained within the control of huge manorial estates. It was this peculiar historical accident that actually made it possible for people like my grandparents to move to Danby and be a part of the community.

The Danby Estate, originally more than six square miles in size, had been given by William the Conqueror to Robert de Brus and passed by marriage down the centuries to the Nevilles. (John Neville married Catherine Parr, later the last wife of Henry VIII.) In the seventeenth century, the estate passed to the Danvers family: one unsubstantiated version of events has Sir John Danvers, a handsome and unprincipled rake of the royal circle, kidnapping and forcing himself upon the heir to the estate, Anne Neville, after her brother and family were mysteriously murdered at home in Wiltshire – a crime for which a parson and a parish clerk were convicted on the evidence of a pot boy, the parson being starved to death on a gibbet and the clerk buried alive. Danvers, it was rumoured, had bad debts and seemed too well informed of the murders not to be implicated.

In 1656, the Danby Estate was put up for sale, divided into 168 lots of farms, cottages and land. In an audacious deal, the bulk of the property was bought by five 'yeomen' of the district. The remaining four lots, which included Danby Castle and twenty-three farms, were purchased by John Dawnay, later Viscount Downe. The asking price was £17,000, around £25 million today if you adjust it to reflect the increase in average incomes. How did they get the money? It seems that the five negotiated with the vendors to buy out the freeholds and sell them to the tenants, paying up when the tenants did. In practice, the process was far from easy: the price seems to have risen to £19,000 and various tenants complained about the means used to assess the value of their purchases. The supposed villain of the piece, Sir John Danvers, was dead before the sale was complete.

The five yeomen became key-holders for an iron-bound chest containing the documents relating to the sale. They all held keys to different locks attached to the chest, ensuring – in principle – that all of them had to be present for the chest to be opened. The documents were scalloped along the edges so that they made up a jigsaw, preventing any theft. The effect of this remarkable deal was to create a large number of freehold properties within the manor and make land available for future development. Freeholders retained common rights over the moorland, including the right to cut heather to make besoms, and to collect endlings – the fallen twigs of heather used to light fires – and the right to graze sheep on the moors and roadsides.

In return, freeholders owed allegiance to the ancient Court Leet, the manorial authority originally granted by the King, control of which had passed to the Dawnay family. Historically, the court could try criminal offences and could even pronounce sentence of hanging. It is still functioning today, meeting each autumn at Danby Castle, a stubby post-Norman sandstone ruin on the narrow twisting road into Fryup Dale. Inside, the ruin is rather well furnished, with a low-ceilinged jury room at the back of which sits the very iron-bound chest that once contained the sale documents for the estate.

These days, the court helps manage relationships between the various moorland interests: the court officers, appointed from among the farmers, keep an eye on the use of common land, impound stray sheep and help resolve boundary disputes. It does have legal powers and an incomer who parks his Range Rover on the common-land grass verge may find to his consternation that he is visited by a couple of lean-faced locals who tell him that he will be liable to a fine from a medieval court.

Sheep are the principal item of business. The Dawnay Estate includes more than 12,000 acres of common land with ancient grazing rights, including four moors – Danby High and Low Moors, Glaisdale Moor and Lealholm Moor – as well as pasture, village greens and roadside verges. All parties want the land grazed, but they have often argued about the intensity of grazing. Grouse-shooting provides valuable revenue to the estate; too much grazing means little cover and tick infestations; too little and the young heather, the food of grouse, is squeezed back by cotton grass, bracken and gorse. These days, the concern is that there are not enough sheep. Things changed during the foot and mouth outbreak of 2001. To either side of Danby, in Westerdale and Fryup, the moorland flocks were slaughtered and many of those farmers who did not give up altogether lost the heart to put sheep there again.

Bramble Carr is one of those freehold properties which in theory still owes allegiance to the court, because the land on which it was built was part of that original sale. My grandparents could probably have laid claim to ancient rights of peat-cutting or besom-making. The availability of freeholds meant that in the eighteenth century many

Quakers moved to Danby; and from the nineteenth century, millionaires from Tyneside and Teesside built large houses. The ICI influence was strong from the 1950s onwards and there were other professionals who commuted to the cities from moorland homes. The various social sets coincided and overlapped in one way or another, through the Glaisdale Hunt, the Danby Tennis Club, or simply the pub – mostly the pub.

In a photograph from the 1960s, my grandparents sit outside the Fox and Hounds on a fine summer evening with a group of locals. There is the avuncular solicitor Hugh Burns and his wife Wendy, the haughty but kind Marianne Kidd who lived with her husband Vincent at the Grange in Danby, and John Fothergill, the millionaire from Teesside. The men, with the exception of my lean grandfather, have swelling paunches. The women, with the exception of my portly grandmother, look like they eat nothing but cigarettes and are wearing purple and blue dresses with sash belts and big shoulders. Dorothy is in black and is looking at the camera with contempt. In her hand is a large glass of brandy.

The picture was taken by Dennis Gray, a neighbour who lived at High Bramble Carr, an ancient, narrow and squat house at the top of the drive. Dennis also worked at ICI, for a civil engineering firm that had a contract at the Wilton works. He was a pixie-faced, shy man in his mid forties; most of the time, you scarcely noticed him. Gray by name, grey by nature they said. His wife Peggy was a gap-toothed, fraught beauty. Both of them drank like fish. Dennis was a keen amateur photographer and had a club going one day a week.

Absent from the picture are the Robinsons, Doctor Bob

and his wife Ruth, my grandparents' closest friends in the village and a couple who I much admired. I remember Bob as a slight, elegantly dishevelled man, with a quiet dry sense of humour, though some of his former patients have a contradictory picture of him as a patrician with a booming voice.

Ruth was a village legend. She ran the home and the surgery, raised six children with little domestic help, cooked for anyone who needed it and many who didn't want it, fielded phone calls, sutured wounds, dispensed emergency help and on one occasion when Bob was out had to extract shotgun pellets from six members of a shooting party who had accidentally been peppered in a grouse butt. When the waiting room was crowded and time was short, she would prowl around, weeding out those who could come back later. One stare from Ruth was enough to make you postpone an appointment.

Everything was done with ferocious energy, and later, she would sit in their upstairs drawing room, knitting and smoking and talking. She could talk the hind leg off a donkey. If she didn't have someone there she would get on the phone. Brenda at Rowantree Farm could take a call from Ruth, put the receiver on the counter and carry on baking. Ruth and my grandmother spent hours on the phone. In later years she often called my mother, who she made look minor league as a talker. Mum remembers staying with Ruth at Ainthorpe House in the 1980s. Bob had long given up and gone to bed, but Ruth carried on an uninterrupted monologue until three in the morning, when she started hoovering the house.

Bob was well known for his diligence in reaching patients in all weathers. There might have been good reasons why he did not mind getting stuck in a snow drift for a few hours.

I am always curious about couples who manage to make a success of their relationships, looking for clues as to how it should be done, but one always ends up finding exceptions to the rules. Ruth and Bob were such eccentrics that I suppose their love could never be imitated, only impersonated. As their children tell it, Ruth was from York, the daughter of a GP. She had been a nurse when she met Bob, then a young doctor, shortly after war broke out. He turned up at York hospital with a paper bag of possessions and a canoe. In London, he had been bombed out of his digs three times and there was an arbitrary quality to what he could retrieve from the rubble.

She was attracted. This doctor was good-looking and intelligent but needed taking in hand. At the time, Ruth was engaged but she had – or so she told her daughters – doubts about her fiancé's knees, an objection that seems typically Ruth in the stress it placed upon a matter that does not much concern other people. After meeting Bob, the doubts about the knees grew. She broke off the engagement and enquired of the hospital registrar about the availability of Dr Robinson. Having secured her quarry, they got engaged quietly and Bob then went away to the war for three years.

He was in Burma with one of Wingate's Chindit columns, fighting the Japanese. Ruth wrote to him three times a week, helpfully keeping him up to date with her busy social life. Periodically, in India and Burma, packets of letters would drop from the grey jungle sky, informing Bob of concerts and dances and family matters in York.

When Bob came back he went first to Preston to visit his mother. Both her sons had gone to war and she had suffered a nervous breakdown and had been hospitalised. Ruth travelled to Lancashire to meet Bob; he told her that she would know when she was coming to the right station because the train passed through a tunnel beforehand. Every time a tunnel came up, she diligently applied her make-up: by the time the train came to Preston the powder was hanging off her in clumps.

When she saw Bob, she cried. He had amoebic dysentery and weighed just six stone. They got married straight away – his family thought he might not live long. Ruth took care of him; the sight of her in full organisational mode must have terrified Death from the room. She had her own approach to a crisis. I had a lecture or two from her myself about how to deal with things. 'Now look,' she told me once, 'if you want to survive in life, you must know how to make chocolate sauce.'

They came to Danby in 1949 by chance, because it was the only vacant practice that Bob could find. It was cold and lonely and remote in those days and the job was physically demanding – the previous doctor, who had died on the job, had allowed himself one week off a year to visit the Scarborough Cricket Festival just a few miles away – but Bob immediately fell in love with Danby.

It was a place that lagged behind. Things came to Danby at least fifty years later than the rest of the world: houses that looked Georgian had been built by the Victorians and moorland life was more in touch with the nineteenth century than the twentieth. Many of Bob's patients had been sent from home to work on neighbouring farms when they were infants, for otherwise they might have starved. One woman had been just ten when she had gone away to work, so small she had to stand on a stool to make bread. She did not see her mother for a year, though she was living just five miles away. For a farmer's wife the work was never-ending. Most of it consisted of feeding men, sometimes having meals on the table six or seven times a day. In the 1940s and 1950s, many farming families never saw a bit of meat from month to month, except rabbit. Mention rabbit-meat to old farmers, and you can see them physically flinch from the memory of how many of the buggers they had to eat when they were kids.

Farms were frequently run by one man. The human body was the only machinery. Men had to manage 16 stone sacks, working until they were in their seventies or eighties. Bob knew one old boy who had carried two full milk churns, each heavier than himself, 50 yards up a steep hill in a foot of snow, every day for six weeks, so that the milk lorry could collect them. Locals walked everywhere. The grocer, Archie Alexander was still doing his round in his eighties, walking the whole of Westerdale by mid morning. The postman, Robert Medd, had an 18-mile round in Danby Dale, during which he had to climb forty-four stiles. In all, he reckoned he had walked 250,000 miles, ten times round the world. Medd tried to finish his round by one o'clock, and did a little insurance work on the side as well as pausing to offer advice on farming and family life. He seemed, Bob noticed, to know the contents of the mail long before it was opened. 'One from Italy,' he would say, or 'all roobish.'

Despite its sense of community, there was plenty of loneliness in Danby: the moors were like a beach on to which was washed up the debris of far-off storms. In 1959, the body of George Baxter was discovered lying on a paper mattress in a boarded-up house in Rosedale where he had lived as a hermit for twenty-five years. Baxter was once a prosperous textile importer and had previously served with the West Yorkshires in the First World War in which his brother had been killed. The war had never left him and eventually he had shut himself away, though he did cut a hole in the boarding so he could be visited by the rats, his former trench companions.

People could become bizarrely isolated. Bob knew a forester who had planted up a wood just three miles from where he lived; he never visited it for the next twenty-five years. The strength of the moorland farmers was in their parochialism and in their attachment to their land, but when their little worlds crumbled through age or family death or debt, they were left isolated, walled up within the self-sufficiency they had painstakingly created. Loneliness and illness were related, interchangeable as cause and effect. Outside the villages, farmers might not see another human for months and made little division between themselves and the animals. During one heavy snowfall, Ruth had to advise a farmer by telephone every fifteen minutes on how to deliver a baby. For him it was easiest to think of his wife as a cow. 'Water's gone, same as cow's', he said, and eventually delivered a healthy boy.

At times, farmers had trouble distinguishing between their machinery and their animals. One local was seen in pursuit of a runaway tractor, shouting 'Whoa! Whoa!' Farm children had a limited vocabulary, but knew droving slang: 'Cush, come on,' they would shout at each other in the playground, or 'Eye opp' or 'Away'.

Women seemed to cope with the isolation better than men and often outlived their husbands. Bob would take the widows with him in his car on his rounds and found that a run-out worked better than a pill. They'd see places and people they'd not seen for years and find some strength again. There were many women who chose to live independent lives up there, some taking the place of the missing son in a farming family. On the moors, the social assumption that a man was a necessary companion became irrelevant. Gender disappeared; one's identity merged with the animals and the land.

People still talk about Lizzie Watson of Haggaback Farm above Commondale. Born in 1850, she managed her parents' farm alone. When she died in 1933, the farm had no running water or electricity while heat came from a turf range that had burned ceaselessly for a century. Lizzie spent the evenings in front of this, with a ram's skull looking down at her.

There were family feuds about tenancies, and disputes with neighbours over boundaries, and stray animals that would be handed down for generations. But everybody was subject to the weather and when the snow fell, they could not choose their friends. In necessity, they helped each other.

Bob found it a good place to recover from his experiences. The war had wounded many people, but unlike my school teacher, Old Hay, suffering had not made a sadist out of Bob, if indeed he had ever had the capacity for cruelty. It made him empathetic. His health never recovered fully from Burma and at times, he suffered from crippling black moods, so he did not discount the maladies of the mind. He knew that depression evolved from numerous factors. It was as individual as its sufferers. You had to live with it, accept to some extent that it was your companion, and sometimes just sit it out, like a ghastly guest you were stuck next to at a life-long dinner party. 'The mysterious disease known as depression classically improves in the afternoon,' he wrote. 'A lady of good works bought a one-way ticket to Whitby more than once, and took a rope in her handbag. She always came back.'

You might spend a lifetime looking for the perfect partner, but the best companion is always laughter.

13

MOONLIGHT

All lasting relationships need an outlet. Life with Ruth could be pretty insufferable at times, so it was as well that Bob Robinson had another love on the go in his enduring fascination with Danby. He never stopped walking the moors, chasing down history and sucking in the air. Standing at Ralph's Cross, up on Westerdale Moor, Bob could look across thousands of years of life engrained in the landscape and feel it was all still alive. His patients would sometimes complain that he was more interested in the history of their farms than the account of their illnesses. Perhaps some of this was a way of dealing with suffering, a constructed bedside manner; chatting about local history made it possible to put a buffer between himself and the present. His vagueness could be annoying. There was one occasion when a retired police officer in Westerdale, who had a habit of shooting at ramblers, locked Bob in his kitchen and would not let him leave until he had gone through a written list of ailments.

Bob wrote everything down. In the course of his thirty years' work in Danby, he compiled enough material for several books; he wanted to produce just one. But what sort of a book was it to be? It turned into a sprawling project with an element of Borges or Perec.

It might have been the memoirs of a moorland doctor, a gently affectionate narrative, like the Dales stories of James Herriot, with people instead of animals, except that people are not as obliging as animals with their comic turns, and a doctor cannot be so loose with his confidences as a vet. There is no confidentiality regarding the treatment of a cow.

Herriot, in reality the Thirsk-based vet Alf Wight, had struck upon the knack of writing about people obliquely, by channelling their characteristics through their animals. You could not be so free or so charming with people if you were a doctor. There was enough material for a novel or two, but Bob did not have the arrogance of a novelist, whose job it is to decide whether his creations live or die.

Bob's pleasure was in the details of life around him, not in any sweeping romantic narrative. He could have written about the evolution of the village or produced a guide to the walks of the area. Instead, he carried on making notes about people, places, views, stone crosses and farms.

In retirement the need to shape this material in some way continued to nag him. He was dying as his daughters typed up the piles of notes into the best order that could be managed. *The Story of Danby* was privately printed in 1991, but it was all a rush and in the end the book was neither one thing nor the other. There were evocative early memories told with flashes of literary confidence, then the book fractured into chapters of notes that had an almost medieval feel to their brevity. The trouble was that there were so many things to say, so many people to mention; everyone seemed of consequence, like Mr Rivis, who had the mill, and was a generous fellow but very deaf. A man spoke into his ear asking him for the loan of a tanner, or sixpence. There was no response, so he asked into the other ear for 2/6d, five times as much. 'Nay,' answered Rivis. 'Go back to my tanner ear.' Bob loved it all and that context to his life sustained him; but in loving less widely he would have had more to say.

The strongest bits of the book were also the most personal – the memories of when he and Ruth first arrived at Danby and the place was still a riddle to be solved, thrilling in its novelty.

It was a winter's evening in 1949 when he and Ruth first drove across Blakey Ridge, coming north past the Lion pub: snow was beginning to fall and the moors were black and white. Sheep were heading down into the villages, huddling around the houses that were humped up with snow, like white cottage loaves. The previous winter the snow had drifted to the tops of telegraph poles and the doctor had visited patients on a carthorse; this time Bob and Ruth were the last people to cross Blakey Ridge for six weeks.

The widow of Bob's predecessor was an invalid and still living at Ainthorpe House. In those days, the long, herringbone sandstone building was held on a tenancy and divided down the middle, with the doctor taking the east wing and a neighbouring farmer the west, the larger portion; the surgery was in the middle. For years the front door had been barred and blocked with a chest as the wind had been too strong to allow it to be opened safely.

The doctor's widow put them up that first night, but the house had rarely entertained guests and there were no curtains in their room. Forty years on, Bob could remember lying in bed, looking through the window at the falling snow. The light of a full moon poured through the glass and fell on him and Ruth. There was moonlight and silence and snow softly falling, the elements of an enchantment that was never lifted.

Later they moved up the road to the Fox and Hounds. Inside, the fire burned big and bright: outside, the pub's sign creaked all night in the wind and the snow-bobbled sheep bleated. Word got round that the new doctor was staying; every time Bob visited the bar he had to put away another round of drinks that had been lined up for him. His patients were showing their appreciation in advance.

When they moved into Ainthorpe House, Ruth arranged to switch ends with the farmer so they had the bigger side and he got to be nearer his farm buildings. From the walls and doors of the farmer's end of the house they pulled out more than 100 six-inch nails which had been used for hanging clothes and harness. They borrowed cutlery and a saucepan, bought a bed, and each evening stayed warm in the inglenook. When spring came and the snow was gone, the previous doctor's possessions were put out on the lawn for auction. Bob bought the surgery couch, chair, instruments, a fine half-skeleton and a 1930 medical directory. He also bought a set of dental tools – there was no local dentist and his predecessor had often had to perform extractions, once even on the train between Danby and Castleton, just a few minutes' ride.

Everyone was engaged in post-war spring cleaning, decorating and furnishing, setting up for a new life. In those days, floors were all varnished black and a fresh layer of brown wallpaper was applied annually. When they renovated Ainthorpe House they discovered nine layers of brown wallpaper. One afternoon, Bob came home to find that Ruth had begun knocking out walls and cupboards to make an upstairs drawing room. I remembered that room from many hours sitting there while Dorothy and Ruth held their conversational marathons. It was warm and light: since then I have wanted an upstairs drawing room, somewhere that you naturally stop on the climb from kitchen to bed.

Bob had 120 farms to look after with an average size of just 40 acres. Half his practice was within two miles, the rest within eight. At Ainthorpe House there was no appointment system, just morning and evening surgeries. Sometimes patients waited twenty minutes, at other times two hours. Mondays and Fridays were busiest. Farmers were led by the weather and if it was sunny or wet the surgery would be quiet. May was a busy month: people would be shut away over the long winters and when the snows thawed and they got out and about again, so did the bugs and mumps and measles.

Bob saw as many people in their homes as in the surgery, so as much effort went into transport as doctoring. A practice of eight miles' radius may not sound much, but in winter, short distances had an epic quality. Bob struggled on through ice and snow, mud and flood. Often he dug or pushed his car out of a drift or a ditch. The district nurse advised him to get as close to the farmhouses as he could, even if it meant getting stuck, as the farmers would pull him out. They did, using tractors and chains and hessian sacks, bracken and even on one occasion a pitchfork, which burst the tyre but allowed the rim of the wheel to grip.

There were all sorts of tricks to getting over the moors. In Westerdale, there was a ford that filled to 18 inches in heavy rain. Bob learned to keep the engine revving fast as he went through in low gear. When the car stalled he would keep it in gear and move it on the starter motor. Small cars were best; forget heavy four-wheel-drive vehicles. You needed a ten-horsepower Ford, with good tyres and a weight in the boot. Going up the moors in snow you selected a low gear and never changed out of it. Small cars could also be lifted out of the ditches by hand. Car radiators took a bashing. The farmers fixed them with chewing gum or oatmeal or cracked a partridge egg in the radiator – the albumen sealed the hole. On freezing, damp, cold mornings when the car refused to start, Ruth would push Bob off down the short drive of Ainthorpe House or he would spray anaesthetic ether into the carburettor.

There was an ambulance service based out towards the coast at Loftus and in winter the drivers performed extraordinary physical feats to stretcher out the desperately sick. Farmers helped, carrying patients in the bucket of a tractor until they could reach a cleared road. Sometimes only Bob could get there; he would leave the car in a blizzard and walk or ski across the drifts to visit patients.

The farmers were contracted to clear the roads with ploughs attached to tractors. There were no tractor cabs in those days, so the drivers wrapped themselves in layers of overcoats and scarves, working with visibility down to a few yards, their clothes thick with ice and snow, just like the fleeces of the sheep. The ploughed snow rose up in walls ten foot either side of the road. If passing places had not been cleared there would be chaos as one driver reversed in the face of an oncoming vehicle only to find another coming up behind. There was no relation between time and distance. A mile or two might seem infinite.

For the first ten years, Bob spent much of his time opening gates. Before the roadsides were fenced and cattle grids installed, the dale roads were gated between fields with the beasts roaming across the road. Each gate had to be opened and then closed, the weary doctor getting out and mounting up each time.

In Westerdale, Bob made numerous visits to a man with bronchial asthma who lived at the end of a track with fourteen gates. Bob had to get in and out of the car fifty-six times to make one complete visit. Well, fifty-eight times if you counted getting in and out of the car at the patient's home – though by the time Bob got there, he was so tired the object of the visit was likely to have been forgotten.

Sometimes it wasn't possible to be scrupulous. Farmers knew that if the cattle were all in one field, someone was very poorly as the doctor was obviously in a hurry. After a while, Bob worked out a way of balancing the open gate on a stone and then whacking it with a stick as he went through, so that it swung shut behind him. It was best to take a passenger to do the opening and closing and from the age of four his children became his gate-openers. By the 1960s, many of the gates had gone and the fields were fenced; the milk lorry was able to visit farms individually instead of collecting churns from the end of the track.

Bob never had much trouble dealing with the beasts. He always took a stick along in case there was a mean-natured dog, though in practice the only one that bit him was a small West Highland terrier. At one farm, bullocks ate his car keys after he had left the window open. 'Don't fret, Doctor. They won't hurt cow,' said the farmer reassuringly when Bob complained.

Few of the farms had phones, though there were phone boxes in some villages and word reached the doctor by informal courier, passed down the dales and over the moors. He was summoned by tractor, sledge and horse. One old lady who lived up Westerdale used to fire a gun out of the window when she needed help. He was often away from the surgery from early morning to late afternoon, seven or eight hours at a time. If he was needed urgently, Ruth would phone the contactable farms in the vicinity of his visit and someone would get on a tractor or horse and go and look for him.

On summer days when he went off walking the moors, Bob would turn regularly to look through his glasses at the distant roof of Ainthorpe House. If there was an emergency, Ruth summoned him by climbing on to the roof and spreading a white sheet across the grey Welsh slates. In 1956, he installed an early answer-phone, on which he left instructions as to where he had gone, and if possible, the telephone number of an adjacent farm. It so delighted locals that they kept phoning up just to hear his voice.

On average he was called out at night twice a month. Out of pride and courtesy, farmers were reluctant to get the doctor out unless the situation was serious, much more reluctant than they would be to call a vet. They often waited until morning before contacting Ainthorpe House. When the night calls came, Bob would roll out of bed and pull on trousers and a wool jersey over his pyjamas. Ruth slept like a log and mostly never realised he was gone until he told her the next morning. One night when

Ruth was away and Bob was alone with the children, he was called out to a farm at Staithes; he tucked two warm and half-asleep children into their dressing gowns and took them along for the ride.

On another late evening call, this time to a pub, Bob was met by the landlord who ushered him quickly to the bar, thick with customers and smoke. 'There's a feller ower there has taken sick,' said the landlord quietly. 'But come and have a whisky first, Dr Bob.'

'What about the sick chap? Where is he?'

The landlord pointed shiftily to the corner, where a figure was propped under his flat cap, a glass in front of him.

'He's well for the minute. There's no hurry.'

The man did not stir when Bob approached. Bob looked at the full pub. It was not hard to work out why there was no hurry – no hurry for the customer nor the landlord – so he sat down next to the dead man and finished his drink.

There was not only ice and snow and flooding, but thick fog that settled on the high moorland where the roads had no markings. Visibility would shrink until the exhausted driver became mesmerised from staring at the verge – his only guide – and was liable to end up in a ditch or rattling off the road down the moorside. In the fog he felt more than just physically lost. It seemed like a complete annihilation of all his bearings. Where the hell was he and how had he come here?

Then spring would arrive, with its fountains of white blackthorn flowers, the dale heads yellow with daffodils, catkins of willow, alder and hazel, maythorn, meadowsweet, buttercups and vetch, wild roses and foxgloves, thirty miles of purple heather, cascades of scarlet rowan berries and finally the red rust of autumn bracken.

This was what he remembered. Most of all, he remembered the moon shining through the naked windows that first night at Ainthorpe House, and how he and Ruth lay in its light while outside, snow softly covered the world; that enchanting snow.

14

COMPLICITY

At the top of the drive that led down to my grandparents' house, up from Bramble Carr Cottage and the big house, was High Bramble Carr, home to Dennis Gray. It was a very old place, parts of it dating back to the seventeenth century. Tucked back from the road, with low doors and small windows, it had a stubbornly discreet look. You'd scarcely notice there was life inside.

Dennis's wife, Peggy, had died of cancer soon after George and Dorothy came to Danby, leaving Dennis to look after their daughter Shelagh. I remember her from those first years I spent at my grandparents'; she was a thin, pretty girl with a shining pale face and often came knocking at the back door, standing in the snow in her thin coat. She must have been in her early teens. Dorothy fed her and taught her to paint. My brother John remembers Shelagh arriving with a set of car keys in her hand. 'Dad's drunk,' she said to Dorothy. 'I've taken his keys. What do I do now?'

I was vaguely aware as a child that Dennis Gray drank, but I didn't then know the full story, or why it was that

Shelagh was regarded with such tenderness throughout the village. I didn't know that I was looking at the remnants of a love story gone wrong, until Shelagh told me.

Both her parents drank, but so long as Peggy was alive, their daughter came first. Peggy had a warm and intelligent heart and was devoted to Shelagh, determined that despite the remote, cold situation, things should be perfect for the child. She cooked and cleaned, gardened and sewed Shelagh's clothes. But, at times, High Bramble Carr must have seemed to her to be a dark and unhappy place. On a winter's night it might be raging black outside, and inside Dennis would take up a poker and thrash the fender. Peggy would take the little girl and hide in bed with her.

Shelagh was just eleven when her mother died; Dennis was hopeless by himself. He said he loved his daughter, but he could not demonstrate it by being sober. She had to look after him: the house became cold and damp, the wallpaper peeling.

Most days, Dennis put on a suit and tie, combed his hair and faced the world, slipping through in his nondescript way. He was a perplexing man, with the ghost of vivacity and a pale spark of passion. He also took a good picture and he left behind thousands of slides of turbulent moorland landscapes, boozy gatherings and women who came and posed for the photography club: Helen, Audrey, Jane, Alison, sitting on drystone walls or gates or in the light cast aslant through some old mullioned window, dressed in purple or fancy lace, their faces slashed with make-up. There are pictures of him laughing, in the embrace of a lively evening, arms round chums. He had a slinky rat-pack quality. He came alive when he had a few inside him, at least, that was the case for years.

Dennis and Peggy were incomers who had moved to Yorkshire after the war. Peggy had served in the WAAF and her discharge book recorded her distinguished service in secret work; Dennis was in the Royal Engineers and left behind his Italy star and his pay slips for Captain Harry Dennis Gray. The war had marked them both. Peggy had done well, and it was often the case for women who served that the return to domestic life afterwards proved disappointing. Dennis did not have a good war.

Towards the end of his life, when he was very ill, he told Ruth Robinson that he had been at Salerno in 1943, a crisis-ridden operation codenamed Avalanche, in which the Allies had attempted to trap the Axis forces in the bottom of the Italian boot. Between mid September and early October, the Allies had suffered 12,500 casualties. Something had happened, Dennis said, at Salerno. Who knew what Dennis had done or not done? What was he thrashing when he went for the fender?

At weekends Dennis lived in the Fox and Hounds or the Duke of Wellington next to Danby Green. He sometimes drank at lunchtime, drove home, parked in the garage, banging the car against the tyres strung along the back wall, and slumped over the wheel, passing out. Come the evening he would wake up, reverse out and head off down to the pub again.

Dennis would feel awful about his behaviour, take Shelagh's hand and weep with regret; but it was his own inconsolable lack he was feeding. Crying and apologising made him feel better – he just could not hold things together without Peggy – but he did not change. A forgiving child is an asset to an alcoholic.

Children are extraordinarily resourceful. A child knows that to survive it must find food and love. Shelagh knew that she also needed some sort of camouflage. There was a crew of hard drinkers who came back to the house, and sometimes when there were men around she felt instinctively that she was in danger. In the end she thinks it was because she was so grubby, and looked so much like a street urchin, that no one touched her.

People knew what was going on. Ruth Robinson, Marianne Kidd and Brenda Tindall all looked out for her, and there was my grandmother down the bottom of the drive. Shelagh always felt safe with Dorothy, sitting there in the kitchen, painting. At my grandparents' children were respected. The community looked after Shelagh, which was the way things were done in those days, though it made everyone complicit in Dennis's addiction. People were less judgemental than they might be today. There were, after all, a lot of people damaged by the war one way or another.

Given the amount of drinking that went on, John and Ilsa Kenney at the Fox and Hounds were pivotal figures in the community and attracted mixed feelings. Ilsa was appreciated for her hospitality and the warmth she showed towards the waifs and strays of the village, but the farmers' wives did not welcome the lock-ins that kept their husbands out till the early hours, and the younger women thought Ilsa was a flirt with their boyfriends, too keen to lean forwards and let them get a good look at what she had on offer. She ran a good pub though.

Ilsa and John had also emerged from the wreckage left by the war, and came north to Danby looking for a place to make a last stand. John was a dentist, who had served in the RAF, and had been told aged forty-seven, that he had lung cancer and six months to live. (He was a chain-smoker, who had a fag in his mouth even when he was shaving.) Ilsa, seventeen years his junior, had previously been engaged to a young RAF officer who died in a raid on Germany. She had wanted to be a singer or a dancer, and John liked to play the piano, so they lived out a show-song romance.

Since John's death was imminent, a reflective change of scenery was sought. The couple saw the Lion at Blakey advertised in the *Yorkshire Post* and drove up to Yorkshire on a whim. On Castleton Rigg they stopped the car to take in the bitter February scene; John essayed a few tentative gulps. 'I can breathe,' he said, to his own surprise. After they took the pub they realised the depth of their ignorance. The Lion was a near derelict mess: chickens and sheep wandered in and out. One day a man turned up with a cow: 'You'll need a cow,' he said. 'They allus had a cow up here.'

John still had a dentistry business in Sheffield and Ilsa was often alone but reluctant to let the locals know. When they offered to buy the new landlord a drink, she would accept and take it to the kitchen where she pretended John was doing the washing-up. One night she ended up with pint glasses lining the kitchen table and thinking it was a pity to waste such nourishing stuff, she gave it to the chickens, who staggered drunkenly back into the bar from which they had recently been driven.

Their two daughters, Jane and Liz, grew up wild, riding

ponies bareback over the moors, impervious to the cold winds, running to and fro between the Lion and the small cottage across the road where, on the scarred lip of Rosedale, lived the widow Mrs Thompson and her stepson Frankie, strong as a horse and as they said locally 'a bit slow'.

Mrs Thompson and Frankie lived off 'sad cake' – puff pastry baked on the range and soused with either treacle or gravy depending on its designation as main course or pudding. The Kenney girls often joined the Thompsons for dinner, before which a goat would be stood on the table and a couple of jugs of milk drawn off into a bowl that was placed under the table, from which both humans and cats helped themselves.

The Kenneys moved down from Blakey just after my grandparents came to Bramble Carr. John left the running of the pub to Ilsa: it was just a business to him. If he had his way, the Fox would scarcely have opened. You knocked on the door and if he knew you, he let you in. Other times, he left the bar untended and you served yourself.

His true love was for his collection of military memorabilia. The collection occupied the top floor of the Fox. I was admitted once, and it was made clear to me that this was a privilege. I was actually quite frightened by the encounter with several man-sized figures in old uniforms: a field-grey German with a spiked helmet and long, naked bayonet; a cavalryman with a plumed head and brocaded jacket with a glittering sabre. What were they doing here, these ghosts of past battles, in the attic of a moorland pub? It was one of the largest collections of military memorabilia in private hands. In the end, in addition to the two thousand cap badges, he had a huge array of uniforms and a fair bit of weaponry acquired one way or another.

John died in 1976, the same year that Dorothy had her second fatal stroke. He had outlived his terminal diagnosis by twenty years. Ilsa left the Fox and sold John's memorabilia to the Imperial War Museum. The truth was that Ilsa disliked the collection; it had been like a field-grey, bloody-handed mistress, devouring their money and John's affection. 'Onward Christian Soldier' reads John's inscription in Danby churchyard; a nice touch.

Ilsa looked after Shelagh Gray from time to time, though both of them found this slightly difficult. Shelagh felt this woman took the money that should be feeding her; Ilsa in turn felt badly for the little girl. She remonstrated with Dennis, but the position of a publican is almost impossible in these circumstances. Are you responsible for an individual's behaviour? After Peggy's death, Ilsa was instrumental in getting Dennis to send Shelagh away to board at a convent in Scarborough, where she thought the girl would be better cared for. It seemed to Shelagh like she was being pushed out of the way. Along with other local children, she made her way back across the moors at weekends and sometimes stayed with friends rather than face her father. She found other things to love. There was an old horse that she stabled with Marianne Kidd at the Grange in Danby and when that died, she moved on to the boys; she was a wild beauty by then. At sixteen she was pregnant by a quiet, kind-natured local lad who later worked for a circus. She kept the baby. She had met the boy down the

Fox and Hounds of course, where she would subsequently meet her first husband, Harry.

The boozing scene at Danby caused ructions between my parents. On the occasions Dad visited, he was likely to gravitate to John Fothergill's house above Danby Green, where the drink flowed freely. 'Fothers', the local millionaire, was chairman of Pickerings Lifts in Stockton. He was no beauty; he had false teeth and made a chattering, slurping noise when he laughed, but he was a kind man and I remember how he used to give the children rides in his open-topped Bentley, and the smell of that cream-coloured leather. It made money seem interesting.

Nearly forty years on, Dad's trips to Fothergill's parties still rankled with my mother. When she talked to me about Fothers I could see from the corner of my eye how my father, who was sitting with us, folded his arms and tensed in anticipation of the attack.

'I didn't enjoy being there when they were getting drunk,' she said to Dad. 'I remember you getting horribly drunk. Completely pissed. You and I had to walk back from there one winter's night when we were staying at Ma and Pa's. They had a caravan then. The children were asleep in the house: we were in the caravan. You were so drunk we got as far as the bottom of the road – the Ainthorpe turning. Outside the doctor's house. There were huge snow drifts. And you fell over and wouldn't get up. I tried to make you but you refused, so I thought, bugger this and walked home without you. I thought I'd give you an hour or so to see if you came back. By three in the morning you hadn't come and I got worried. I thought you might have frozen to death. So I got Pa up. George wasn't pleased. We went looking all the way down the road. Not a sign of you. Very worried. We came back to Bramble Carr and heard a strange humming. You had come back and gone and climbed into the car in the garage – they had a garage in those days, it was sold and became the gardener's cottage – and started the engine. Gone to sleep. God knows how you didn't die.'

Dad smiled ruefully. I had long realised that booze was an issue in the family, and that when it comes to drinking in the family, you are all involved. Dad had always been more relaxed for a beer or two, and as boys the happiest times we had with him were when we were on a boat or at a cricket match and he was cracking open a tin. 'Don't tell your mother,' he would say, when we stopped at a pub on the way back home. 'You know what she's like. Have a shandy.' There were pretty pubs in those days, in Lincolnshire lanes that had scarcely any traffic and where the walls were hung with honeysuckle. Most of the land-lords were ex-RAF men, solid fellows wearing blue sleeveless sweaters. Over the bar would be pictures of the Dambusters, the Lancaster squadron who had been based nearby at the Petwood Hotel in Woodhall Spa. When we began drinking ourselves, we realised quickly that our presence permitted Dad to open a second, then a third bottle.

He retired early from the RAF, disillusioned. He was an excellent pilot, courageous and ideally suited to action, but the only plane the Lightning ever shot down was a stray Meteor trainer and Dad was in desk jobs the latter part of his career. He did well when he could stomach his superiors, but in the 1980s he got into trouble after some duty-free fiddling was discovered on his watch. For a while it looked as though he might be made the scapegoat. He came to visit me at Oxford, his hair falling out with the stress. I took him to a pub on the river. 'It's been going on for years, this business,' he said to me. 'It's the shit that holds things together. Why me?'

He wasn't made the fall guy but it was the final straw. After he retired, he had a sort of breakdown, secretly, in his loft, where under the pretence of running a business framing prints, he drank. He was in his early fifties: his hair grew back and he was handsome and fit, clever with his hands and knowledgeable about plants and furniture. He had the chance to start again. Instead, free of the RAF discipline he had loathed, he lost his direction. He attended one job interview and when he narrowly missed out he never applied for another job. At my house, he once left a notebook, on the front of which my mother had written: 'A man of action – his plans for action.' Inside, it was blank except for a drafted letter complaining about a local planning application, and notes for how to deal with his parents' estate when they should die, an event eagerly looked forward to, though in this he was long frustrated as his father died aged ninety-eight and his mother made it to one hundred and one, by which time there was little money left. Motivated by Mum he would have a burst of energy: build, dig, plant, then go back to the pub.

I can remember how they were sitting when we talked about Fothergill. It looked just as usual. Mum was at one end of the kitchen table, her back to the chimney breast, hidden around the corner. Dad sat with his back to the window, facing all doors. Nothing would come in without him seeing it. This was how they had sat in that house for twenty years while they talked and argued and some-times laughed. After her stroke in 2009, Mum said she wanted to stop fighting, but she had so many barbed memories, to which Dad now had no riposte. What could he do to change the past? I remember that he was wearing a brown fleece jacket and his arms were tightly crossed and his lips pursed. I felt for him; he was lonely. I thought of how I had found him, when I was a boy, sitting vacantly in an armchair under one low lightbulb, a look of animal confusion on his face. I had put 'Help!' by The Beatles on the record player. 'I like this song,' he had suddenly blurted out.

Mum didn't know that Dad was ill. He knew probably, but refused to recognise it: he said he was just having trouble swallowing. He still drank though. He was rarely a staggering drunk, but alcohol was always necessary. 'Very relaxing,' he would say as he had a first drink.

What was the cause of his tension? His own father, Air Vice Marshal John Le Mesurier Cohu, had been a manipulative brute who had physically and emotionally thrashed his two sons as he groomed them for the RAF. Dad was disobedient and though he was the elder son, he had been supplanted in his father's hopes and affections by his younger brother Jeremy. It was a burden to be the favoured son, and gentle Jeremy suffered, but still my father was jealous, and admitted that he treated Jeremy awfully when they were young. Dad's mother, a sweet, bullied woman always known as Bobby, had supplied my father with all the love she could on the sly, mostly in the form of food, hence my father's constant obsession with what would be on the table. Bobby had a bad time with John, too, as he regularly disappeared with a mistress, and left her alone in their remote Devon house, even when her sight was failing. John liked to squeeze a thigh and in the early years of my parents' marriage, he took a creepy interest in my mother; on one bizarre occasion, he knelt in front of her, grasped her legs, wept and protested that she was too good for his son. We learned later that John himself had been the child of alcoholics, had been effectively orphaned and never knew what had happened to his mother.

For years, my grandfather wrote my father letters that began 'Dear Monster'. Our rare family holidays in Devon inevitably ended in near brawls, with my grandfather shouting at my father 'D'you want a punch up the nose, youngster?' He once chased Dad from the house with a shotgun. Despite which, when Jeremy died tragically young, my father hoped the funeral would provide the opportunity for reconciliation. I saw it all; I guessed he was going to try it, and I knew what would happen. I shook my head at him, and then covered my eyes. My father tried to embrace his wizened, wicked little father, who publicly pushed him away with contempt. After that, I felt I could forgive Dad the drink. I could forgive him most things. In fact, it made me want several drinks myself.

15

THE NIGHTINGALE

After her father's death, Shelagh continued to live at High Bramble Carr, through two marriages and three children, scarcely removing an object from the house, until it was cluttered with the past, with books and china and pictures and photographs. In time, she put herself through the Open University, did a degree and a dissertation and went into counselling. It was a revelation to me that she had pulled through that childhood and made something of herself, when others I had known, who had none of her obstacles, had fallen along the way.

What always surprised me was the lack of bitterness she showed when talking about the past. She had a way of describing what had happened that put her in the picture, that pale child, but did not make her the whole story. She was sympathetic to her young self, but she also seemed understanding of the adults in the story, fair to them sometimes beyond what was fair for herself. I suppose that was because she knew that everyone in her story was a child to one degree or another, and stuck that way forever.

All of us have known people who have been inconsolably hurt by life and often it seems impossible to say that the responsibility does not lie with a particular individual. But having reached that understanding, what is one to do with it? You can imagine, as my father did when he reached out to embrace his own father, that everything could be made right with a piece of theatre, some public ceremony of reconciliation. In Dad's case it went horribly wrong and simply reinforced his hurt; as a picture of his situation it could not have been more articulate.

My eldest brother, Nick, who had the most detached relationship with my father and saw least of my parents because he was away at school from the age of seven, attempted to stage a similar scene with Dad. Nick had been a precocious, sensitive, clever child and should never have been sent away to boarding school so young, although this was quite a common arrangement for children whose parents were in the forces. He suffered as a consequence, particularly in his relationship with his father, and had great difficulty in getting beyond those early experiences. From being a young child he had a freakish knowledge of classical music and opera and it seemed to me that down the years, no matter how well he was doing, he was always waiting for the curtain to rise on his life – that before he could really begin there would have to be some sort of transfiguring, artistic experience.

Inevitably, he decided he would have to confront Dad, and of all the unjust things that had been done to him, he picked on one specific, almost insignificant incident that he thought exemplified his problems. Once, when he had been miserable at school and no more than ten years old, he had been desperate to speak to his parents and had called home from a pay phone, asking the operator to reverse the charges. He heard my father answer, and then he heard him decline to accept the reverse charge call. He talked about this incident continually, and convinced himself that if he could exact an apology from Dad, then everything else would be set right; that time would shift and adjust and wipe out all the mistakes. The magic spell would be broken and his real life would begin.

My brother John and I warned him against it; we knew Dad better, but Nick persisted. He planned the scene; he waited until my mother was away, he cooked for my father, as she would have done and then raised the matter of the phone call. Dad could not remember it. That was all he said: I have no recollection of what you are talking about. What do you expect me to say? Nick was devastated, but confirmed in his hurt, and so the search continued for a critical moment in the past drama, a moment that could explain everything that he felt had gone wrong.

Things would not have been any different if my father had broken down and wept in apology. Blame constrains us and makes us the puppets of remote circumstances. Nick was in a muddle, and there was little that my father could do about that. Increasingly music took the place of other relationships in Nick's life: it might have seemed emotionally sustaining, but it left him self-preoccupied and isolated. Music was the echo of his own feelings.

In an odd coincidence, as I was nearing the end of this book, I was talking to a musician friend about the wolf pit and its metaphoric significance for me, when he said, 'It makes me think of Weber's opera *Der Freischütz*.' I felt a small shiver, because I remembered that Weber's opera, often translated as *The Marksman*, is among Nick's favourite pieces of music; he often played me the famous scene in which a diabolic contract is made in a terrible place known as the Wolf's Glen, or Wolf's Ravine, in the presence of Samiel, the Black Huntsman. The opera ends happily though, with scenes of reconciliation and forgiveness and a new life for its young lovers. In my choice of the book's central image, there was probably the thought of the wolf's glen and an unconscious acknowledgement of my brother's dilemma, as well as a note to myself about the perils of a certain kind of romanticism.

Surviving entails forgiving and finding a way to admire the view over the past, no matter what desolation it contains. In the boxes stored in her house, Shelagh found an explanation as to why things had gone so wrong at home and was able to put her relationship with her parents in some sort of context. At the back of a cupboard under the stairs was her mother's crumbling diary, much water-stained and damaged, in which Peggy had written irregular entries between her teenage years in the 1930s and her middle age in 1959. There were also papers that showed that both Dennis and Peggy had been married previously. From these a story can be pieced together, the ripples of an intense love affair that had petered out on the moors.

Peggy was the daughter of Edgar Burdett, headmaster of the French Protestant School in Soho who had married into a well-off Belgian family in the fabric trade, so she had Belgian blood as well as Welsh. She was brought up in Surrey, liked boys and had a lot of fun before she went into the WAAF and married Lieutenant Colonel Edmund Lewis Rowlands. 'Rowley' was later the boss at a Wiltshire engineering firm when Dennis Gray came to work there. Dennis was married and had a daughter, but within a few years, he and Rowlands had run off with each other's wives. It led to a double divorce, but the courts moved slowly and by the time Dennis and Peggy were able to marry in 1954 they had perhaps been lovers for five or six years. Such affairs were not common in the 1950s, and it made them social outsiders. Dennis's job on Teesside, at the other end of the country, represented an exile and seems to have been arranged by Rowlands. Peggy and Dennis were escaping to the moors with their boats burned.

The drink rotted their shared life; still, from Peggy's diaries it is clear that she had been in love, not just with Dennis, but again and again down the years. Love was her true addiction and what had forced her hand in life. Without the feeling of being in love, life was meaningless.

Her early diaries are a debate as to who she loves and who really loves her and which of Ray, Ken, Harry, Peter, Tom or George offered the best combination of brains, looks and prospects. One kissed well, another was hand-some, a third had big shoulders and was charming. One, who she hoped to marry, died suddenly. She was not lucky in love and even when she had what she wanted, she was full of regrets for what might have been. Marriage to Rowley gave her financial security but lacked passion, at least on her part, and she wrote longingly about the other men she had passed by, relationships that might have been consuming enough to keep her faithful. The diary tailed off.

Then, at forty-three, after a fourteen-year gap in writing, she turned again to her diary: 'What a silly little bitch I was all those years ago,' she wrote. 'And yet I can remember how desperately uncertain I was of myself really and worried that perhaps no one would ever really want to marry me at all.' She was happy now with Dennis, she wrote 'perhaps for the first time as really happy as nature will allow'.

She and her husband were still lovers and she so loved her daughter, though she did miss the nice things she had enjoyed with Rowley and wondered if 'there is some awful streak of discontent in me that I seem powerless to overcome'.

Among the pages of the diary was a love letter to someone, written far back in the 1930s and never sent:

It is such a divine night. The whole world seems flooded with moonlight . . . The trees in their first leaves cast strange intricate designs on the dew-wet grass. In the hollow by the wood the shadows deepen and the mist reaches out phantom fingers. Through the open window I can hear a nightingale trilling.

Only the nightingale and I are sleepless in this sleeping fairyland – a night created for those who love, but you my darling are so far away. With your arms around me the wistful song of the nightingale would be a poem of joy . . . we would reach the enchanted realm of love.

Shelagh recalled that as a child she once went into the garage and caught her mother in a clinch with John Fothergill. Peggy the young poetess had dreamed of the enchanted realm of love: she had a gift with words and a luminous honesty. But, as for so many of the women in this story, what place was there for her in the world?

Perhaps love became her creative outlet, when she was able to free her energy and imagination. In the end she had a cold cottage on the moors, a drunken husband and a middle-aged grope with the local Mr Toad. But she couldn't help herself. Love retained its integrity, and though it led her into all sorts of duplicitous situations, it seemed to her that she was pursuing the truth. Beyond the empty bottles was a woman terrified of disappearing if she stopped feeling.

My sister Lucy once said to me that one of the contradictions of ageing was that you felt relieved to be free of the ghastly fluctuating emotions of youth, but there came a point when you were frightened you would never feel anything at all. Then you were dangerous to yourself and others because you simply wanted to feel again, to feel anything, so that you could feel young. You struggled to overcome emotions, but without them, the world seemed dead.

After my first encounter with romantic misery, which left me floundering on the moorside, I hoped never to experience it again. I reasoned that romantic love was dependent on a popular false equation: I love you, therefore you must love me, with love being an uncertain value, but generally to do with slavish exclusivity.

To love this way meant either putting your sense of self in another's hands, and risking losing yourself entirely, or demanding of them an impossible exchange and being disappointed at their refusal to acquiesce to this one-sided bargain. Either way, it seemed an impersonal process.

Love – whatever it was – had nothing to do with the day-to-day world. If you wanted a partner, you needed a mutually considerate arrangement of friendship and sex. That would do.

Despite my intentions, I did fall in love again. The consequences were not as disastrous as before, but there was a predictable pattern to events and to the torrent of feelings that they unlocked, so much so that I came to think that falling in love was inevitably the re-enactment of some significant crisis. Unlike my brother, I did not see it in terms of a single event, but I had certainly had some experience that had made me determined to be emotionally self-sufficient, even though I was temperamentally highly emotional, so that when I lost control of circumstances, the emotional response was disproportionate.

In my twenties self-sufficiency was an important part of the way I saw myself. I remember how much I admired those Yorkshire farmers of my childhood, because they seemed so self-sufficient. Yet even they were liable to go off the rails when their defences failed. I was proud of the independence I cultivated as a teenager and had worked hard to build a personal myth of my detachment. The hitch-hiking was an important part of this.

It began when I was fifteen. After Dorothy died, Bramble Carr disappeared as a refuge for the school exeats and half-terms. It was very rare for us to go home except during the principal holidays, so I was thrown back first on Tart's hospitality then on school friends. Since I hated the feeling of dependency, I took to hitch-hiking. I did a trial run to visit Tart one weekend and when that went well, I began to drop in on family friends and relations throughout the north, then went national. For my last three years at school, I lied systematically to my housemaster and my parents about what I was up to. Mum did ask sometimes where I was staying, but my parents had encouraged this independence, so it was no good complaining when I edited out chunks of my life. The school took my word as to my destination. 'Staying with family friends,' I would say, or 'going to an aunt'.

I put my clothes in a rucksack, stuck out my thumb and hitched to York, Sheffield, Stratford, Cambridge, Oxford and Brighton. I often went down the A1 to London, where my eldest brother Nick was at university, living in a succession of dingy places in south London.

I kept the phone numbers of potential hosts in a little black notebook, and called them at the last possible moment to warn them of my arrival. By presenting myself as a figure in transit, I put myself outside definition. I couldn't be an imposition: there was even a touch of romance to my fleeting figure.

The journey was always more important than the destination. Though it was often boring, it could be enhanced by gambling. Standing in a lay-by, or on the slip-road of a service station or off a roundabout on the A1, looking at the darkening sky and at my watch, I would calculate the chances of reaching a suitable berth before night fell. Winter, when days were short, was tough. In summer, if you set off early enough from Barnard Castle, you could be pretty sure of making London in ten hours. I often hitched at night but only once did I have to sleep rough – under the hedge of a vicarage in Sunderland.

You had to be early at the Mill Hill roundabout in London if you wanted to avoid the queue of hitchers. I always stuck to the major routes: cross-country hitching was hard. A service area was better than a roundabout, the latter better than a junction. I learned never to stand too close to a slip-road entrance. Give the driver time to see you and think yes-no-yes-why-not? Look them in the eye; stick your thumb out like you mean it, and smile. If a single driver selected you from a waiting queue, you declined the lift. It would be one of those men whose hands strayed from the gear stick on to your knee. If you found yourself in a car with a creep, you asked to be dropped immediately or threatened to open the door. You never let on that you were a schoolboy. I had a map and memorised the route; I never accepted an unjustified detour.

Many of the drivers who picked me up had hitched themselves. Others were commuters, salesmen and truck drivers. They wanted to talk, to relieve the boredom, so I became good at listening and asking.

Progress between London and Scotch Corner was never continuous, never smooth. Time stalled or fled. Hitching time was time distorted by location, by regional temperament, by traffic habits. Time slowed down near the gravitational pull of large cities: you could be stuck in their looming, yearning shadow, while away from the towns the empty countryside flew past.

Getting out of London was hard. There was so much competition and the cars and trucks were fast out of the blocks. Eighty miles up the road, at the Little Chef near the Peterborough turn-off, people had calmed down. Further north, beyond the cooling towers of the Ferrybridge power station near Pontefract the drivers were more local, off to Leeds or York or Darlington. There were more options for travel.

The light changed going north, from pallid, anxious grey over London suburbs, through the wobbling watery skies of Cambridgeshire to the long low northern light. It was light with a stain of varnish in it and over some far, western horizon, a flourish of purple and red.

I often got lifts from miners coming off shift. Going up and down that road, I rubbed shoulders with the cities my grandparents had come from.

Sometimes I ended up back at school when it was still shut. When the school was locked there was a window in the changing rooms next to the shower block that could be opened from the outside, but mostly there was a door or two open as masters and other staff came and went during the holidays. No one noticed. The rest of the world had been wiped out by a plague and only my footsteps echoed where a thousand feet ran every day.

Up and down the road I went, up and down, in a busy limbo, building up my solitary resistance. So long as I had to keep moving, to reach some destination before the sun went down, there was no way that I could feel morose. Of course I resented my parents. It seemed outrageous that those who insisted they love you should deny you access to them. How could my mother be so loving and then so inaccessible? She made you feel like you were the centre of her world, and then she turned back to her preoccupying relationship with Dad. I knew there were practical reasons, but every time I went up and down the A1, I was scribbling another line through my parents' names.

Future attachments were always fraught with the possibility of failure; I hitch-hiked through life. Then came the actress, the reversal of roles, and the abrupt withdrawal of affection which unlocked all that neediness. Despite my schoolmasterly instruction to myself that there would be no recurrence of such feelings, they did come back. As I got older, I said I wanted to feel less, but I was desperate to feel more.

I am told that the Eskimos have thirty different words for love, which makes a mockery of our conformist romance industry, selling its vague, prettified ideas of self-less union. Each one of us has our own experience of love, and it is rarely a simple equation of two halves making a whole. For me, love generally began with a shared walk on the moors, in a wood or on a chalk-dusted down, where I would revisit, in a way, the solitary hitch-hiking world, but this time I would not be alone.

The presence of a lover reclaimed the past and it would be as if the world had shone into me through a lens and set a fire alight. There would be the scent of heather flowers, or bluebells, or wild thyme and life felt raw and vivid: one feeling sparked another, until all semblance of cause or order had gone and the lover became utterly, selfishly essential to my feelings.

It was exhausting; strange how emotions, abstract and intangible, have such violent physical effects. A friend who dismissed love all as hormones and adrenalin collapsed after a love affair: the French doctor she saw told her that she had a broken heart. Apparently the stress does cause muscular strain on the heart, so whether love is a chemical or a story, the effect is the same.

Far easier to settle on mutual desire as an objective; but if you have fantastic sex, it leads to the not unreasonable assumption that the relationship ought to develop, or you'll lose the sex, instead of which desire is suffocated by tender domesticity. On the other hand, what is companionship without desire? Love is the mortality of sex, but sex is the morality within love; it will find out a fake. Infatuation is like fireworks after the field is deserted, with no one but you to see the display. The beginning and the end of an affair are the parts that are remembered, the selfish parts of navel-gazing emotion, the hideous, glorious times when nothing else in the world matters but your excitement or your loss, even the times when you feel that you have been thrown to the wolves and are being torn apart.

It is often little to do with happiness and is an obstacle to life. When the emotion had burned out, I would actually feel happier, more stable, and promise myself that it would never happen again. One struggles to describe romantic love in terms that do not seem drastically destructive or drearily banal. Language can give shape to the most abstract ideas and elevated ideals, but the building blocks of romantic love are mostly everyday elements with their natures reversed: tenderness with the sudden capacity for anger, affection that is raw with the anticipation of refusal. Break the passion into its component ingredients and one becomes horribly aware that the bonfire is made of the contents of the kitchen cupboard.

After a while, I'd feel there was something missing; the nightingale; that enchanted realm, and the fire that would burn everything up.

16

THE GOOD SHEPHERD

Slipped inside a book I was lent by Shelagh, I found a newspaper cutting from October 1990, showing a picture of Frank Raw's last sheep drive from Great Fryup Dale to the market that used to take place in Danby. He walks down through Fryup on a crisp October morning, drystone walls and languid ash trees to either side, crook in hand, while behind him follows a frothing column of white sheep with black faces, filling every inch of the road. Uncannily, the column looks to be walking to heel, forming a tidy trotting line to Frank's rear: it is as if he is the leader of a marching band, about to give his stick a twirl.

I remember seeing the sheep drive as a child. It is a memory of being stuck in the car with George while a vast bleating procession bobbed by, but I don't remember Frank. My grandmother knew his wife Enid through the Fryup WI, a rather elite branch of the Institute for which Dorothy did backdrops and displays. Enid told me that despite the caption, the man in the picture is not Frank, but his brother Martin. Frank was probably chivvying along the rear of the column, doing the mucky business; he did this drive every autumn for thirty-two years, bringing 600 ewes, gimmers, wethers and shearlings down to market. (A gimmer is a ewe that has not yet borne a lamb; a wether is a castrated ram lamb; a shearling is a sheep of either sex that has not yet been shorn.)

The drive was six miles but took two days and brought the area to a standstill. It was not universally popular. Frank was just fifty-seven when he packed it in. His hips were giving him trouble and everyone else was moving sheep in trailers and trucks, so he did the same, though he still thought that the sheep were better for the walk. There was something about that mammoth procession, something ceremonial: it was the shepherd's moment, and the sheep's too, when they did a valedictory parade through the landscape they had shaped and when everything had to stop for them, and bugger them if they did not like it.

I love seeing shepherds at work: it is such a practical art, but an art nonetheless, to be able to move these animals to and fro as if you held them on a piece of string. As kids, we used to watch *One Man and His Dog* on the television. I held my breath as Phil Drabble quietly commented on the tense moments when a collie would stop and crouch and slink in response to the shepherd's call, and then all at once, the sheep, hesitating on the edge of the gates, would go into the fold. It was magical to see how a man could extend himself and turn his thoughts to action by using a dog. When I moved to Lincolnshire I got a small flock of sheep myself in the end and had a lot of fun looking after them, but I never had a collie. Instead, I found the most reliable means of catching them was to train them to come to a bucket of food. No skill, just greed, which does an effective job, but by then I had seen a lot of bad sheepdogs too.

Danby farmers say that there is no one left who knew sheep like Frank, no better shepherd. He often said that sheep were maggot magnets that knew a thousand and one ways to die. But there was something about the business that got him. Sheep are infuriating to the point that you simply have to get the better of the buggers. They are all different and yet all the same, changing minute to minute, driven at times by canny consideration, at other times by blind panic. Isn't that really very human?

When he was young Frank had not intended to farm. He came from Ajalon Farm up Fryup Dale, where seven generations of Raws had farmed – probably eight now, or nine. They have been there pretty much since wicked Sir John was said to have got into trouble and flogged the Danby Estate. Frank said that farming was a daft business and the boys of the family stayed because they lacked the initiative to be elsewhere. Then he damaged his right arm too badly to do National Service, went shepherding in Northumberland and got into sheep.

When he came back to Yorkshire he married Enid, who was working as a nurse in Leeds, and in 1958 bought Dale Head Farm, which was then just the land and a ruin, with 318 acres and the grazing rights on the moors. He began with just eighteen sheep, Scottish Blackfaces, then added Swaledales. Some breeds were bright; some infinitely stupid. Moorland sheep may produce only one lamb as a natural response to upland conditions, hence moorland ewes are put to a lowland ram so that they will produce pairs of lambs and a more maternal lowland streak will, one hopes, be introduced into the breed. Like many others, Frank crossed Scottish Blackfaces and Swaledales with lowland Bluefaced Leicesters to produce so-called Mules. Lowland sheep have no moorland sense. 'Sheep have a habit of dying,' he said. 'But the Bluefaced Leicester tup has developed this into a fine art.' Some of that art of dying entered the cross-breeds. He lost sheep on the roads and in the bogs, in the snow, especially when that twenty got stuck under the ice up on the moors. Another time, they were victims of their own good sense. He lost sixteen – he could tell, even passing among the thousand-odd, that he was short – and thought they must have been rustled by villains from Middlesbrough. Searching for them, he passed several times by a remote shooting lodge but did not think to look inside. Eventually someone tried to open the lodge door and it stuck against a carcass. A local lad had been taking a girl up there and had left the door open. The sheep had gone in for shelter, blundered about and shut the door behind them, then died of thirst. He hated that; it was the worst sort of death and all because some kid wanted a shag. But then, that was life.

Until I had sheep of my own, I was puzzled as to how sheep were allowed to roam free of boundaries in this vast space. You could see they had been marked here and there with splodges of spray paint, and latterly ear tags, but how on earth a farmer knew where to find his sheep baffled me. What prevented them from wandering fifty or a hundred miles? Sheep have a tendency to 'heft' themselves to a particular territory: they become attached to a restricted area and regard it as a secure home from which they are unlikely to stray, even if there are no physical boundaries. I kept mine behind electric fences that they constantly tested, but when I removed the wire and tried to persuade the sheep to cross into different pasture, they simply would not go. They were unconstrained, but persisted in grazing the edges of their former perimeter as if there was an impregnable barrier.

Moorland sheep have to be hefted to the farmer's moorland grazing. It can take a few years to impart that knowledge to the flock. The shepherd has to be with them every day: eventually the ewes know the area and teach their lambs the boundaries, where to find cotton grass and water, how to avoid the bogs and where to shelter. Even then, you can't heft sheep successfully unless there are other flocks to their flanks. Sheep stick to their own flocks and don't mix, so the presence of strangers all around ensures that the sheep stay put.

The whole business of moorland grazing is interdependent. It needs every farmer to participate fully. When the puzzle no longer works, when one piece is missing, the flocks begin to wander into the gaps. Without neighbours who are also strangers, the fabric of this sheep-society begins to fall to bits. When the sheep began to disappear from the moors, the few that remained were more likely to stray than the many there had been.

'Hefting' is a word full of quiet wonder. You can teach a creature to respect invisible boundaries: you can create in it a notion of home in a wilderness and you can compel order in this arrangement by keeping the various parties strangers to each other. It seems contrary to all natural instincts.

Frank reckoned that it took an acre to an acre-and-a-half to support each sheep, so his flock might spread over fifteen hundred acres and it would take him three days to round them up, walking, or in later years, riding. He had three dogs and Enid would drive up to switch the dogs when they were exhausted. You had to know the moors to round up: you had to know the heather and the bog, the escarpments, pits, howes and grouse butts, all the inflections of colour and light, all the optical illusions of this purple and black and brown landscape in its various moods. Without that intimacy with each curve and subtle horizon, you hadn't a clue which way the sheep were being driven. There might be no sun to guide you, no wind to test; you could wind up in Glaisdale or on Blakey.

When it was all working, he was one man and a dog moving a thousand sheep across the moors, twitching them here and there, doing that magic. Then he'd get them down and sort out those that had strayed from another heft. In the old days there were many nicks and burned horn markings to distinguish each farm and flock: his marking books showed how Raws in Fryup had been marking their sheep in the nineteenth century. In the 1980s, he still had a V nicked into the underbit of an ear and FR on both horns.

Sheep farming was always poor work. You were at the mercy of subsidy, the weather, disease or the carelessness of visitors. Sheep-farmers were blamed for most of the moorland problems, for depredation, ticks and worms: the estate or the conservation authorities would be at you for this or that, chivvying you off the moors and then they'd suddenly be asking where you'd gone. The incomers who liked the way sheep grazed the village changed their minds when a few ate the hedge or got into the garden. Sheep-farmers, they said, rarely went to heaven. You needed good neighbours if you kept sheep and the humans had to be well hefted too.

All the same, it was seen as honest, even romantic work, something with a distinct value to it, a way that man connected to the environment. For me, the idea of the good shepherd had an irresistible biblical glow. A good shepherd was a good father, but the metaphor should not be taken as a literal instruction in parenting. Farmers of any sort end up having to put their animals before their nearest and dearest. Being a good shepherd often means being an absent father. Even in my small way, with my thirty or forty sheep, which I had got partly to please my wife and kids, I found myself falling foul of my family because I had to go here or there to care for the sheep, instead of being available to them.

Everyone likes a lamb, but such cuteness has to be paid for with work. Still, when the rest of life's problems seemed intractable, spending time with the sheep was a way to avoid the complications, and as the silences grew at home, I spent more and time in the company of my ruminants, ruminating on how things had come to this pass.

Fryup is one of the loveliest of settings for a dale farm: the big villages of Danby, Glaisdale and Lealholm are nearby but Fryup retains a singular isolation, a green silence, and seems full of secret space and leisurely echoes. The roads are narrow, the sides of the dale are steep and the bottom flat. It is enclosed and hidden, protected. In the middle of the dale, curled up like a dog in a basket, is a long green hill, known as Heads. The hill divides the dale into Great and Little Fryup dales and has the disorientating effect of blending in with the background, so that you quickly lose your bearings and this small dale seems vast.

In the 1970s and 1980s the Raws' pretty farm hosted school trips and days out for young offenders. Enid has pictures of them all, the young coming to learn about the craft of the shepherd. But by the early 1980s, Frank was feeling unwell. He wondered if it was something to do with the new dips they had to treat sheep scab.

Sheep scab is one of the severest of the many diseases of sheep. It is a form of dermatitis that results as a reaction to the parasitic scab mite which lays eggs in the fleece of the sheep. After hatching, the larval mites become adults within a fortnight, feeding on the surface of the sheep's skin and causing an allergic reaction that damages wool, depletes the ewes and stunts the growth of lambs. Scab had been eradicated in the 1950s, but reappeared twenty years later. In 1976, the Ministry of Agriculture ordered all sheep-farmers to dip their flocks twice a year in organophosphate-based pesticides that were effective against sheep scab, ticks and flies.

In Fryup, Frank had particular problems with tick infestations. Since this had an impact on the grouse and irked the Dawnay Estate, he dipped three times a year rather than twice. He did the dipping with his brother, but began to have odd reactions. His face would swell up and turn red and he would tingle and feel numb. Eventually, he ended up in Middlesbrough General Hospital after collapsing with an acute reaction: he was sweating like a pig, his skin was covered in weals and he had a vicious pain in his kidneys.

Frank's experience was not unique. Sheep-farmers all over Britain reported a range of health problems: tiredness, irritability, loss of concentration, cramps, diarrhoea, skin rashes, and chronic fatigue, the so-called 'dipper's flu'. In some cases there was severe depression. The possibility that exposure to agricultural organophosphates can cause health problems has been bitterly debated for more than thirty years without any conclusive result. On the one hand, there is a mass of anecdotal and medical material about individual cases that shows a correlation between incidences of chronic fatigue and exposure to organophosphates; on the other hand, the manufacturers have argued that while the products are toxic, so are many other substances to which farmers are exposed, and that you may only find an association between the symptoms and the product and not an exclusive causal link. Chronic sickness and organophosphates are in the same room but are not necessarily related. This is a version which, broadly speaking, the government has supported. Follow the precautions, and you will be safe, though the use of organophosphates is no longer obligatory.

Organophosphates are a huge chemical family. An organophosphate is a chemical compound of phosphoric acid: naturally occurring organophosphates, such as DNA, are the stuff of human life. Commercially, phosphoric acid is particularly useful due to the ease with which it bonds diverse chemical groups to create potent compounds which are readily absorbed by living organisms. Since their widespread introduction after the Second World War, organophosphates have been effective against fruit flies and mosquitoes, have saved agricultural production and many human lives, and were considered an environmental boon – after the initial hit they degrade quickly unlike the old compounds such as DDT.

In biological terms organophosphates work so well because they switch off production of an enzyme, acetylcholinesterase, which enables nerve function in both insects and humans. Inevitably, chemical multinationals have been interested in phosphoric compounds for the way they might kill men as well as benefit them. ICI's great rival, the German IG Farben led the way in the 1930s, producing a range of phosphorous-based nerve agents which the Americans later inherited as the spoils of war. In 1954, ICI marketed an organophosphate pesticide called Amiton. It was aimed at mites but was soon withdrawn and is said to have subsequently found a use as a basis for the V Agent chemical weapons developed in the government facilities at Porton Down.

Aspirin in the wrong dose can kill; that a substance is toxic does not mean it is always harmful. With phosphorous compounds, it is the cumulative effect that is at issue. Today, the use of organophosphates is so widespread that their role is being questioned in everything from the collapse of bee populations to the rise of ADHD in children, suggesting that in certain contexts even small amounts may be poisonous. Most of us still regularly use various kinds of organophosphates around the house in flysprays and weedkillers and though these are carefully designed to avoid harm to humans, they are not altogether safe.

Back in the 1970s, when farmers were using tubs of the really rough stuff, there were regulations – more in the way of guidelines – for usage, requiring workers to wear bibs, facemasks, rubber boots and gloves when dipping sheep, but there was no enforcement and in practice, it was so hot under the kit and so hard to handle the sheep wearing all the rubber that self-protection was often disregarded.

In the pictures Enid has you can see that they tried to take precautions: broad-shouldered fellows with mutton chops and long 1970s hair hanging over their collars splash around in oilskins and aprons and gloves. But they did not wear facemasks and had no idea of what they were dealing with. The pesticides could penetrate any area of skin they touched and while some people seemed to be able to cope with the effects, others were floored. The Countess of Mar, who has been a long-standing champion of farmers claiming to have been affected by dipper's flu, says her own problems started when sheep-dip splashed into one of her wellie-boots.

When Frank realised that he was suffering, he stopped doing dipping himself, and just did the round-up. But even the smell of the dip would make him swell and tingle, and the dip lingered on the fleeces. He had to admit that it worked well, though. He rarely had any problems with ticks once they began using the dips. They worked like magic, Enid remembers. The chemical world which my grandfather prowled, smoking his pipe and fiddling with molecules, brought into the working lives of farmers a mass of practical benefits: herbicides and pesticides that tidied up imbalances between man and nature and seemed to square the circle.

After the foot and mouth epidemic, Frank retired and sold Dale Head Farm. He and Enid retreated to Raven Hill, a solid, former gamekeeper's cottage that sits in Fryup Dale. It has thick walls and is inhabited by a solid silence; in the background the wind thumps, like a heartbeat.

By then, Frank had developed a number of allergies, some of them connected with dyestuffs or preservatives. In January of 2004, when there was a power cut in bad weather, he and Enid got together with neighbours to make the best of the situation, each of them bringing along whatever food was left post-Christmas. Frank nibbled at a few Brazil nuts and subsequently thought he was suffering a recurrence of the dipping symptoms. He swelled up, his lips went numb and he felt poorly. He went down to see the doctor in the morning, came back home, collapsed and died of cardiac failure. He was just seventy. His family had generally lived into their eighties or nineties. 'We had made our wills,' says Enid, 'but I wasn't expecting him to die.'

Most Brazil nuts are sprayed with organophosphate pesticides, but that proves nothing. In fiction, I might be able to bring some justice to Frank's death, prove a cause and track down the perpetrators. But this is a life story, a thread of inconclusive anecdote, and one is left with a sense of unfairness, of how life punishes those who follow the instructions on the tin. The people who do as they are told are treated with cynicism; let the good shepherd have his reward in heaven.

The sheep had been disappearing from the moors even before the foot and mouth outbreak. Without them, the moorland changed character. The sheep had sculpted the environment, pushed back the undergrowth, lifted the branches of the trees. They cleared channels of hunger and curiosity, opening up the vistas of stone walls and distant farms so beloved by visitors. Now the views are different. Along Danby Rigg, above Rowantree Farm, little stands of rowans are shooting up, scrambling through the bracken and spreading towards the heather. Rowantree Farm does in fact possess an ancient, twisted rowan, just on its boundaries. Behind that tree, its offspring, scattered by the birds, are rising in a line. Rowans love the acidic soil. If there were no intervention, this moorside would soon be a mass of red berries and scarlet leaves in autumn and beautiful in quite a different way. Today, if I sit on Danby Rigg, in the same place I have sat often down the years, the gorse has grown head high and I can no longer see the roof of Bramble Carr Cottage

17

ABANDONMENT

The last time I visited my grandparents' house was in the summer of 1980. George was sitting in the kitchen, as he always had done, his back to the door, the yellow overhead light shining down on the blue Formica-topped table, newspaper and home-brew to hand. He was slower, his movements less sure. He harrumphed more. He offered me some beer: it was awful stuff by then, his Geordie brew, weak, yellow as bile and fizzy as pop, made in filthy bottles and drunk too young.

Robert was there too. He had bought a little house in Durham where he lived when he wasn't at sea and had been taking a bit of time off to catch up with George. He was on edge, pacing up and down the kitchen behind his father who seemed to cower in his presence. Robert was in one of his large phases then, shaggy and bearded and bellied from booze, wearing some stretched and shapeless knitted number. He was drinking black coffee and chain-smoking Benson and Hedges, sucking at the cigarettes until they went soggy and straight away sparking another.

George harrumphed; 'You want to be careful about the

great number of fags you are smoking,' he said, turning his head slightly so that he could see something of his youngest son, but not all of him. Robert put on a display of exaggerated pathos: 'Oh, leave it out, Pa, I've already given up the booze. I've got to have something left.' He went and made himself another cup of coffee. George sipped his beer. I sat by the pantry door. There was still a lingering smell of Kitty Kat, but no flour or sugar.

I don't remember much about the visit beyond the sight of the father and son having this strange conversation, the father staring at the table, the son staring at the back of his father's head. The place was implausible without Dorothy, but she couldn't be mentioned. George did not like to hear her name. He seemed to regard it as an outrage that she had in some way abandoned him.

I later learned that George had lost his driving licence. He had gone to visit Robert in Durham one night, had drunk too much and ignored Robert's plea for him to stay. Outside Durham, he was caught by the police going the wrong way around a roundabout.

My aunt Rose was living not far from Danby, keeping a close eye on George, though she was by then widowed with three children and a full-time job. From what Rose says, it seems that Robert had a crazy idea that he might stay in England and look after George, but his father was not receptive to the idea. Shortly afterwards, Robert left for Australia and I never saw him again.

For a few years, George lingered on at Bramble Carr. People were fond of Dr Brooks and in winter the grocer from Castleton used to walk over to Bramble Carr with a knapsack of essentials. Frank Farrow, the butcher from Danby, took him his piece of steak. They noticed that George was becoming temperamentally peculiar, physically unco-ordinated and oddly lupine in his looks. When his younger grandchildren visited, he pulled horrible faces at them.

At first, it was assumed that he was depressed, the natural consequence of being old and lonely. He had previously suffered a bout of depression prior to his retire-ment from ICI. At the time the subject was avoided, but after his death, it turned out that many people guessed that when Dorothy had complained about George's deep-ening silence, her husband had been having a profound personal crisis.

Work had sheltered George from his inadequacies at home, but with retirement looming, his work would soon be over. It had not led to any great change in his personal fortunes, not had his work ultimately been enduring. ICI was struggling with its own health problems; his intel-lectual excitement at being at the technological forefront had been replaced by the awareness that the world had an insatiable appetite for novelty rather than a desire to change its constituent parts and become a more reasonable place.

It was a classic late-middle-aged crisis, common enough when retirement marks a watershed. But it was new then. George's generation were among the first to deal with the existential issues posed by a pensioned-off last portion of their lives. How were you to live without a job, when you had managed, as it were, to exist personally by simultan-eously saying yes to your employer and no to your wife, in one area denying yourself, in the other area denying others? He had failed, or he had been cheated. Maybe, given his silent, hate-filled relationship with his father, he had felt that he would never be good enough anyway.

There was no one to talk to in those days except the doctor, so Bob Robinson was the only person who ever knew what George had on his mind. He talked with George for hours. Bob, though younger than George, had seen terrible things in the war and had a degree of experience that was beyond George. Did he give him the officer talk, about pulling his socks up and getting on with it? Perhaps he just listened. I imagine George sitting there, in silence, lighting and relighting his pipe, struggling to find words for his feelings.

The worst of the depression lifted, but the silence remained, and with it came another kind of retreat. George gradually stopped walking. He had been used to taking off all day across the moors, but at Bramble Carr, with the wilderness at the end of the garden, he eventually found it hard to make himself cross the stile, as if there was something out there that he feared.

George's sadness had not gone unremarked. Ilsa Kenney often used to spot George sitting in the bar during the day, in front of the window with a half-pint, tall and hawk-lean, a pall of sadness mixing with the smoke that circled slowly over him. She would sit next to him for a few minutes; she would even take his hand in hers and they would sit together in silence. He glanced up and made an embarrassed, throaty harrumph, but he did not take his hand away.

His final decline began not long after my last visit to Bramble Carr. It was the optician who first noticed that something was very wrong with George. He had been having trouble seeing, bending low over *The Times* crossword. The optician saw that there was damage to the optical nerve at the back of an eye and recommended he had some tests.

The diagnosis was a long time coming, but it turned out that he had Steele-Richardson-Olszewski syndrome, or progressive supranuclear palsy. PSP attacks deep-seated clusters of nerve cells that govern breathing, eye movement and muscle coordination; it inevitably and irreversibly shuts down the cradle of the mind.

There is little knowledge about its causes and no cure. It seems to predominantly affect men of late middle age and can be present for years before the symptoms become clear. God knows how long it had been gnawing away at George, and what had been mistaken for truculence or cruelty on his part – those faces he pulled at the kids – was probably an aspect of the disease. It might have been present when Dorothy was still alive.

Sometimes PSP is mistaken for Parkinson's, but unlike Parkinson's, sufferers do not shake or stoop. Rather, they seem to go rigid. Emotions may become erratic, but on the whole the brain remains relatively unscarred, intact and even contemplative while the neurological system around it shuts down, cell by cell. Eventually the conscious ness is imprisoned in a frame of useless bone and flesh, a mind staring out through the bars of the body. The stare is characteristic – fixed, sunken, level and unblinking, like a stuffed animal.

Eye movement becomes involuntary; sufferers cannot adjust when they are attempting to climb stairs. They lean backwards, struggling to look upwards and ahead; they lean backwards further and further the higher they go, and then they fall over backwards as if the world had tilted on its side, or they are hamsters who have outrun the wheel.

George began to fall regularly. Sometimes he was convinced that he had cancer and was terrified. At other times, he would say: 'Why couldn't I simply have got cancer?' His 'harrumph' became a low growl. From his cavernous, shrunken face his blue eyes stared, unblinking and blank.

It was a terrible end. His death in 1986 came as a relief. By then, Bramble Carr had already been sold to provide for the constant care he needed.

Over the moors George's employer ICI, fabricator of the modern world, the empire of explosives, fertiliser, Perspex and polythene, came to its own demise in a puddle of raspberry yoghurt.

Things had never been better for ICI than in the 1950s when it enjoyed the luxury of allocating its products to hungry customers. Then competition re-emerged: the world's plastics sector overproduced, leading to a slump in the market. The same happened with artificial fibres – ICI produced both Terylene and Crimplene – and there was a recession in the heavy chemicals market which remained the basis of ICI's business.

Fortunately, in its mad, diverse way, the company was creating a future for itself. In the early 1960s, the paints division launched a tide of Dulux Brilliant White on the houses of England to be followed in time by thousands of shades of apple and rose. Meanwhile, ICI chemists had come up with Fluothane, the brand name for the anaesthetic halothane which replaced ether and chloroform; they also invented the first effective treatment against malaria, Paludrine. Later, they would create the beta-blockers, Inderal and Tenormin. ICI was also busy in the agrochemicals market, dabbling with organophosphates and producing the best-selling pesticide Gramoxone.

In 1989, ICI made a profit of £1.5 billion. But, with its continuing involvement in bulk chemicals, the company was always vulnerable to manufacturing cycles and oil prices. Just two years later, its fortunes were on the slide. It survived an aggressive take-over bid from the corporate raider Jim Hanson, who wanted to get his hands on the profitable pharmaceutical arm but its own shareholders then put pressure on the company to spin off the pharmaceutical and agrochemical arms to form Zeneca and Syngenta. Those who took options in Zeneca cashed in; over the next decade, Zeneca shares traded at five times their initial value, while without the cash-cow of the pharmaceuticals, the shares of ICI scarcely shifted in price.

ICI tried to move away from its unprofitable chemical heritage and concentrate on artificial flavours, fragrances and paints. In keeping with the age of the Sunday supplement, the company was making a transition from alkathene and ammonia to a-hint-of-lavender toilet fresheners and magnolia paint, from substance to mere smell. It hoped to be a ghost of its former self. But it could not dispose of its old factories. It wanted to sell them as one package, but the sale took fifty separate deals spanning years and each time one piece of the chemical production-line went, it made the rest of the package less coherent. ICI was left with an assortment of zombie companies that it had trouble giving away.

One by one, the lights went out on Teesside. By 2003, the dirty past had gone and the situation was beginning to look better for ICI. Then came disaster. A subsidiary factory in Holland produced artificial flavours for yoghurts, biscuits and ice-creams – the plant made 400 variations of strawberry flavour alone. When a software error occurred, the wrong flavours began coming out. Strawberry yoghurts tasted of raspberry. The company lost 20% of its business and its share price plummeted. Soon afterwards it was discovery there was a pension-pot deficit of more than £800 million. The vultures began circling and eventually Azko Nobel, the Crown paint manufacturer, brought what remained of ICI.

On 7 January 2008, ICI's shares were de-listed; the company was formally buried. In Britain, the ICI name vanished altogether, though it is still used in Asia and Australia where the brand is respected because of its imperial past. All that effort and ingenuity and vast industrial power, all those plastic dreams, had come and gone within eighty years, leaving behind rows of spectral, derelict factories on Teesside.

ICI is not the only industry to have faded from the area. There were past glory days for shipbuilding and steel on Teesside, and the moors, too, are marked by the debris of quixotic endeavours, though it took me a while to realise the extent to which industry played its part in shaping the land.

West of Danby, in a fold of the hills, is Hob Hole, a popular spot with visitors, with a pretty ford over Baysdale Beck and a little waterfall. Rising above it is Kempswithen Heights, a ridge of land scored by the sharp grid of a drainage system.

I often walked this way to Baysdale and wondered what modern conservation effort the drains indicated – perhaps they were attempting to stabilise one of the ancient bogs up there? When I eventually did some reading, I discovered I had the wrong end of the stick. The drainage system is all that remains of an eighteenth-century attempt at land improvement – which we would now call environmental destruction – launched by Sir Charles Turner of Kildale, who attempted to turn 600 hundred acres of wet moorland into arable land and pasture.

It was a bold Georgian project. The drains were dug to run the water into Sleddale and Baysdale becks and lime was carted in to neutralise the naturally acid soil. But in fiddling with the status quo, Turner inadvertently created a volatile and unsustainable environment. Superficially tough, the moorland is tender as ripe fruit and minor damage to the surface layer of peat initiates a rapid process of disintegration. The lime was repeatedly washed away and Kempswithen was abandoned after Turner's death. His efforts were replicated on a small scale throughout the moors, where 'intakes' mark the remains of upland enclosures that have reverted to wilderness.

There was a long history of mining – for coal, ironstone and jet. In the eighteenth century coal mined at Danby was hauled by pony and cart to fuel lime kilns in Commondale. Moorland coal was poor quality and costly, and mining was in decline by the early nineteenth century, about the time that the mills of Teesside developed a voracious appetite for ironstone.

In 1853, ironstone was found at Hollins Farm in Rosedale. On Blakey Ridge, next to the Lion, you can stand at the extreme northerly lip of Rosedale, a pronounced, narrow dip that opens spectacularly into the dale sheltering the prosperous village and Abbey far below. There is little human noise, apart from the odd passing car – more frequent in summer – descending north along Castleton Rigg, puttering down into a blue-green wobbling haze of skyline and distant pasture. There are curlews and distant cows and the wind hissing through the heather.

A short, stumbling walk down Rosedale brings you to the route of the ironstone railway, uncannily preserved and marked at points by brick arches set into the moorside. A hundred and fifty years ago this remote place was the site of a huge mining and smelting operation. Up on the wind-struck landscape, with its vistas of blue sky and land-locked stains of purple and black and down among the curves of pastured dale and alder-lined becks were planted the elements of a great industrial scheme. Under the magic influence of the railways spreading out from Teesside, the resources of the area were to be united to form a new city.

The dale belched fumes: it was thick with pits, spoil heaps and kilns. Blast furnaces were built at Grosmont, Glaisdale and even down at Beck Hole (which seems an implausibly cosy nook in which to base such an operation). In 1873, half a million tons of ironstone was hauled up from Rosedale; the same year Austria dumped the silver standard, precipitating a run on the markets and a massive economic slump. A miserable six-year depression followed, weeding out many speculative dreams. Industry retreated from the moors to the coast and the ironstone mines went the way of the coal mines, blending in with the bracken and heather.

Even the solitude of the moors has been a valuable commodity, something that was recognised by the monastic Christianity that first flowed into Yorkshire from Iona. The subsequent influx of monastic orders was led by the Cistercians, whose appreciation of solitude was matched by undeniable industry. In no time at all, huge swathes of solitude had been 'assarted' by the monasteries. Through the Cistercian system of lay brethren – those monks who had not taken orders and could labour outside the monasteries, living in 'granges' and working for their keep – the abbeys developed into profitable communities. In the twelfth century, the Cistercian community at Rievaulx had 140 monks and 500 lay brothers. Yet, even before Henry VIII took against them, the great monasteries were in decline, retreating from the moors like those before them. The cheap labour they needed was no longer readily available after the ravages of various pandemics. The monks left behind flagged moorland paths and stone crosses among the Bronze Age burial howes and standing stones. The pagan and Christian are side by side here, both believers, neither one a conqueror.

The moors have been repeatedly altered by humans whose attempts to wring wealth from this inhospitable landscape have left it scarred with roads, walls, ditches and ruins. These intrusions form the cross-hatching on the picture, the small details that shape ones's impression of the whole. A standing stone or cross breaks the curve of the horizon, looking like some isolated, brooding traveller: the straight line of an abandoned railway cuts across the moors like a sudden quick thought but fades out in an old spoil heap. You are never far from the remains of someone's dream, from the exquisite melancholy of abandonment.

18

HOME

In November 2010, I visited my uncle Bill in Australia, expecting a bit of sunshine. It rained every day of my stay. For the previous decade the country had been gripped by the Big Dry, one of the longest droughts in its history. Fires had torn through the bush of Victoria and the skyline rumbled with smoke. Not this time; I left England in the throes of an early and cold winter, parking my car in the snow at Heathrow, and arrived in Victoria where everything was lush as a Yorkshire spring.

Bill lives in the hills that surround the town of Bright in the Australian Alps. Long, dragon-like ridges line the horizon, red sandstone outcrops, covered with eucalyptus and pine and smoky with wisps of mist and rain. Bright is a pretty place, a gentrified wild-west outpost with wooden store fronts and covered sidewalks. The town meanders among meadows – paddocks the Aussies call them – where kangaroos hop like vast rabbits, from trees to grass and back. The roads are shaded by ash and turkey oak and down the main street of Bright stand old elms of a stature now vanished from England. In the rain it was almost like Hutton Lowcross: just everything a bit bigger. Those kangaroos made me look twice. The meadow grass was full of fritillaries. The morning chorus came with currawongs and kookaburras.

Up here, German immigrants created Australia's first ski-slope, so the place has always been a destination for those with a European yearning. Strange the way that immigrants sculpt the familiar out of unfamiliar ingredients and create a web of association that closes on them. Then they have to move on again.

It is a big sporting destination. Up behind Bill's house, on a ridge called Mystic is a paragliding launch pad, a huge Astroturf pad that curves away over the steep lip of a hill. From here you can inflate the canopy, run, launch, pick up a thermal, and slide through the sky the better part of a hundred kilometres and back. It's like hitching: over each little hill you stop and hang around and stick your thumb out for a thermal.

Bill caught the paragliding bug ten years ago. 'It's a very gentle business,' he says. 'Very gentle.' His father dreamed of flying, of jumping from mountain to mountain. Bill jumps off mountains, floats, glides, curls around and ascends. He regularly goes off with his girlfriend Pip on paragliding trips round the mountains of Europe. Pip watches these days; she paints instead.

Bill is in his mid sixties now, fit, stocky, barrel-chested and moving a bit as I do, slightly stooped. He has a way of talking while rubbing his head in a self-effacing way, contradicting the confidence he otherwise shows. His skin has suffered badly from the sun. His lips at times look oddly green. You can't see far into his blue eyes. He listens closely to what he says, scrutinising it for signs of maudlin infection. Gloom won't sneak up on him, like it did his brother. Guilt and regret exist, but he is determined they should not dominate the story. You have to live in the present, which means having a version of the past that is alive with doubt, not closed with condemnation.

At the top of the Mystic launch site is an automated weather station that you can contact by walkie-talkie. Speaking in a synthesised woman's voice, it gives the wind speed and direction; paragliders call it 'the bitch'. Bill was determined to take me for a flight and every morning he would stand in his pyjamas under the covered porch; 'We'll just see what the bitch says,' he would say, walkie-talkie in hand. 'I'll squawk the bitch.' Every morning she said the same thing in her synthesised voice: wind, rain, no flying. So we sat and watched the rain and talked about what it was like to grow up all at sea.

For those first years on the ships he was reminded constantly how naïve he was; how he didn't fit in. On his first journey they were entering the Bay of Biscay and doing maintenance topside when some rusted bolts had to be knocked off and Bill was sent to the engineer to get a cold chisel. Bill didn't know what a cold chisel was: what with the business over his accent and his natural awkwardness, he was consumed with anxiety about doing the right thing. He held the chisel the engineer gave him; it was hot topside and the chisel felt warm in his hand. Was it too warm? Would he be shouted at? 'Do you think the chisel is cold enough?' he asked the engineer.

The engineer took it back with gravity. 'You know, you might be bloody right,' he said. 'It could mebbe do with a bit more chillin'.'

'Yes, yes. If you think so.'

'Well, we want to get this right first time, don't we?'

'Yes. A cold chisel should be properly cold.'

'Look, to be on the safe side, why don't you take it down to the freezer engineer and see what he can do about it?'

Bill took the chisel down to the chief freezer engineer and explained the problem. The man stroked his chin, while suffering some strange contortion of his mouth.

'Is everything all right?' asked Bill, anxiously. 'Can something be done?'

'Of course, mate. I see there might be a problem with this chisel. It's not that cold is it? But, tell you what, let's shove it on the evaporator unit for a bit.' So he put the cold chisel on the evaporator and Bill watched it sitting there, vibrating and turning white with a metallic hoar frost.

'That looks pretty cold now, mate,' said the engineer. 'You take that topside.' He did. Not for one minute was he allowed to forget it.

It was odd that Bill shared George's interest in science, but that he had no practical inclination. Instead of mechanics, he had learned to finger the violin. In contrast to his father, he also felt that that there was some guiding spirit in life. God was watching out. Religious faith was not, in Bill's case, an assurance of moral propriety but he believed that things tended, one way or another, to work out for the best and that love was reciprocated on the metaphysical level. He feels differently now.

First, there was Robert's death. It was very hard to get over that, but Bill clung on to his faith, until in 1994 his eldest son, Joseph, was electrocuted on board ship when he incorrectly disconnected a 440v supply. Joe ignored safety procedures and was careless, though he only did what all the crew did regularly – except that on this occasion he was unlucky. There is a picture of Joe in Bill's office, lithe and bearded, with that serious forehead and delicate mouth of the Brooks men. Joe is playing the guitar and harmonica using a brace at a party he had organised for the skipper of his ship. Four days later he was dead.

After Joe's death Bill sank into a twilit world of rage and despair, self-pity and grief, sitting late by himself, night after night, drinking. Why? What had Joe done to deserve this? Why this? Rob's suicide had been shocking but there had been a context there: the death was a consequence of depression – of a disease. But Joe's death was without cause or reason. There were days and days of feeling nothing at all, absolutely nothing. There was no taste, no smell, no pleasure, no light.

It was eventually the voice of Bill's father that saved him, though it was spoken not by the ghost of George but by my aunt Mary, who as a child had been George's favourite and who was most like him in her detached exterior and secret tenderness.

'Now then, William,' she said. 'Let us consider the circumstances. You have to decide which way you are to go. Joseph is dead. You cannot bring him back by your grief. And this being the case, what is to be next?'

If he made no choice, that in itself was a defining choice. If he did not care, then he was good as dead. He eased away from the drink. It was still many months before he was able to wake up, look out of the window at the sunlight on the leaves and think that this was pretty. It was years before he could divest himself of his sense of responsibility for Joe's death. What could he have done? He brought the boy into the world. Then, a moment of foolishness had taken him away. It was not his fault. It did not mean he should stop living, quite the reverse. But he never again felt that he was owed happiness.

It surprised me to discover that Bill was never that keen on sailing. The sea did not have any mystic attraction for him. Sometimes, in the North Atlantic or off East Africa there might be thirty-metre swells, huge, slow-moving seas, mountains of green and grey, streaked with spume like quartz, with intervals of a quarter of a mile. The ship would slowly climb each immense wave and meander down the other side. He felt lucky to witness this, but there was rarely any excitement or great danger. The container ships he sailed could easily ride these slow oceanic behemoths.

It was much more dangerous when the wave-length shortened and you got a nasty wind whipping it up so that the ship straddled two waves: then the ship would be held at either end while the water fell beneath it and it would start flexing, shuddering through every steel plate.

A big ship mostly sailed itself. What really interested Bill about sailing was the theatre within the ship, the art of managing men, and the constricted space of the decks where people were defined. Going to sea was a voyage inwards; he was looking for an identity.

His first reports as a cadet were awful. He was a know-all know-nothing with a big mouth. But he never gave up, never backed down and he was bright when he wasn't being dumb, so they persevered with him. There was no easy ride. An Australian merchant navy ship of that era was riddled with conflict, much of it centred on the seamen's union. Officers regularly found their authority questioned, often physically, by monumental greasers. The ship-owners had acquiesced and the men even had their own bars below deck. Bill found that it was impossible to maintain authority and be liked. Sometimes he knew he was hated, but at least he kept the ship. Keeping the ship means retaining the respect of the crew. A first mate or skipper who lost the ship was done for; your confidence was gone and your career was probably shot, too. You had to show the bastards that if it came down to it, if they went for you, you'd stand up. You had to act bigger than you were; bigger, rougher, tougher. But by then Bill had been taking lessons in how to be an Aussie.

Bill first visited Australia when he was just seventeen, in 1963. Five years later he was back to stay. No one cared about social class or how you spoke: all his old anxieties about who he was vanished. He was the other side of the world from his mother and her notions of self-improvement. Doncaster or Danby, the terraced artisan or the pseudo-squirearchy: none of it mattered in this new world. In Australia men drove six-litre cars with crates of beer in the back. You could chuck your stuff in the car, drive a hundred clicks down the road into the desert and camp. They threw 16oz steaks on the barbecue. And they earned real money; a second officer in the Aussie merchant navy could earn one-and-half times the salary a skipper earned in the British merchant navy.

He worked six months on ship and six months off. On shore, he went to work as a painter and docker, right down among the bogans, the authentic Aussie working class from immigrant Scots and Irish families. That was his objective, to go straight down and be accepted as a Philistine among the Philistines, to shed all that snobbish bullshit. To be himself, whatever that was. He lived in Adelaide, then moved up country, falling in with a hippy scene in the Snowy Mountains. By then he had married Barbie – Bill had an appetite for conflict that was near insatiable, but in her, he gorged himself. After a while he began to get bored of smoking dope with the hippies; when he started doing the washing-up, that was it. They said he was making them feel bad.

He and Barbie came across a deserted farmhouse that an old farmer let them have for eight dollars a week. They cleaned the place up, stripped the wainscot, put down woven rush matting and hide rugs. It looked beautiful. A couple of years later, the old boy sold up to a local farmer called Teddy Fraser, who had no problem with them staying. Bill insisted on putting up the rent to fifteen dollars a week and began to help on the farm with the fencing and the sheep shearing and the slaughtering.

There began his true love affair with the Australians. This was the love that he had had been forbidden in England, the backwards affection for the past his mother was determined that her children should leave behind.

He had gone all the way to Australia where he could become – like so many generations of his parents' families – a painter, labourer and now a farmer. Through his respect for the men he worked with, he began to discover the self-love that would replace the nerve that he had survived off. He adored those Aussie farmers – their kindness, their naked honesty and acceptance, their lack of pretension and their obstinate courage. He found their simplicity holy, their patience superhuman.

Teddy had a polio-afflicted brother, John, who farmed by himself. 'Look, mate,' said Teddy. 'When you see him, you're not to offer him any help. Never offer to help.'

That first meeting, they drove for miles across a dark and weary, empty landscape and came across John, alone with a concrete mixer and formwork, casting concrete fence-posts in the middle of nowhere. He had restricted movement in his upper limbs and his hands were tightly clenched, but he was smiling as he worked.

John was Bill's hero. He almost cries when he talks about him. He epitomised all that Bill admired. There he was, in the middle of nowhere, with his locked, twisted limbs and smile, casting concrete fence-posts. Not a shred of self-pity.

Bill and Barbie lived for ten years in the Snowy Mountains, the happiest time in his life. But they now had two sons, Joseph and Luke, and they had adopted another boy, Matthew, from Bangladesh. When Bill was away at sea, Barbie would be up in the mountains with the kids by herself, and it wasn't working. So they came down to Devonport, Tasmania, where Bill was sailing from; and it was there that Robert came to live with them.

Of all the things that have happened to Bill, the subject of Robert is the one that still makes him clam up. 'I honestly don't know what made Robert go into the navy,' he says. 'It wasn't the thing for him.' His bottom lip curls up towards his nose, in painful reflection. 'Look, the thing is, I am still terribly unhappy about Robert. I have a suspicion that in some way I was responsible.' Bill has wracked himself about this, and yet by his own rational argument he was not responsible. Consider the myriad factors that go into the making of such a tragedy: the family history, the chemistry, the genes, the circumstances, the accidents, the drugs and booze.

Still, it is easier to accept responsibility than to admit defeat and say you just don't know why this thing happened, that an inexplicable blackness devoured someone you loved. Love has a weight surely? It is composed of physical things, of gestures, of the pressure of a hand or arms, of words and time and patience, of life forgone elsewhere so that love can be shown. Why then did it weigh nothing compared to the hole inside Robert? It was that blackness that got to Bill, that solid void. He and Rob would be laughing, walking, talking and he'd be on top form and then they'd get back inside and Robert would slump again and sit with a cloud over him. He could not feel anything, nothing inside whatsoever.

Bill would apply his father's brand of reason: 'So: let us consider what is or is not the case. Is there a job? Yes. Is there money? Yes. Is there the prospect of loving relations? Yes. A house? Yes. Then where is the reason for the emptiness? Whence comes the darkness?' This reason saved Bill when Joe died. But it could not save Robert. He would go silent. The shadow settled on his face. He sat, sucking at his fags, one after another, the ash burning red-hot to the filter.

Bill's face sets in numb sadness. 'He was a lovely, lovely bloke. But he had this thing, like it was all Ma and Pa's fault. They didn't do this and they didn't do that. But they loved him. They did. After a long time, if a person is so negative, what can you do? You say, well, if that's all there is, if there is nothing else, just misery, then, bring it on. Let's get on with it.' I have heard others say the same thing, after years of dealing with depressed or addicted partners or family. You want to end it all? Why don't you just get on with it, then? Coping with someone in that state, you can feel as if you are being sucked down – as if their objective is to destroy everything around them. All that matters is their need. If you feel that way, and nothing I try can change it, then go on then, destroy yourself; but why destroy me, too?

I wondered if Robert was gay. Older gay guys I talked to seemed to recognise some of the narrative: the painful bond to his mother, his super-masculine exterior, the self-destruction that ran parallel to his need for a domestic refuge. He gave himself with a romantic desperation that must have frightened off the women he wanted. It was either sheer immaturity, or self-sabotage. It might have been possible he was gay, Bill agrees. But he gave no clue of that. If he had been gay no one would have minded. Dorothy would have accepted him. There was no doubt about that. Or would she? Was her liberality so straightforward, or would she have become all Doncaster about it? George too?

For Bill, the death of Rob, then Joe were not all the grief he suffered. The third blow was the death of Matthew, the adopted Bangladeshi son. He grew up happily but things became stickier after the divorce. Bill and Barbie had different ideas about child-rearing. He thought she was too harsh; she thought him too liberal. Bill wasn't around all the time – he had to go to sea – and the lad slipped into using dope and drink.

After Joe's death, Bill gave a chunk of the insurance payout to Luke and Matthew. He kicks himself about it now. He thought they'd use it sensibly. What a fool he was! Luke was OK, but Matthew spent the lot on strong skunk.

In the mid 1990s, Matthew came over to England and stayed with me. By then I had left the theatre and was working as a journalist. I had smoked plenty of dope at university and many of my working colleagues self-medicated, so I was strictly non-judgemental about drugs, but I could see things were wrong. Matthew spent a week or so sleeping on the floor of my flat. He couldn't face going out much. I left food there, but he made himself cold polenta and lay, stoned, listening to Belinda Carlisle. He was sweet, inarticulate and helpless: the wiring was shorting all over the place. Whatever Australia had offered the white boy from Yorkshire, it was utterly wrong for this gentle Asian-born kid.

That was a few years before the end – years of drugs, booze and increasing mental problems. Matthew trained as a chef, worked in Tasmania and when Bill went down he would sober up and cook for him. He was lovely, Bill said, just lovely. When Bill was gone, he'd go back on the dope again. He took to carrying a knife. Bill tried, as he had with his brother, to pull him back from the brink, but in the end Matthew got out of his head and cut his own throat.

Bill walks on up through the woods, massive shoulders stooped: I am amazed at how he carries the weight of the past. Again, I find myself wondering how it is that some people are able to survive, and again, I come back to the knack that Bill – or Shelagh – has, of telling a story, without putting themselves at the centre. No one is at the centre of the story: life is a web of narratives and there are no absolute causes. It is the natural thing when you are young to be absolute, to see only one colour. When life goes wrong, you have to take it all to bits, and assemble from those redundant pipes and wires what you need to live. You need art, but you also need the pragmatic skills that only life teaches.

Bill has never stopped running ships. His other son, Luke, as bright and charming as his brother Joe, also followed Bill into the merchant navy. Luke is every inch the Aussie hunk. He does a bit of modelling on the side and became the surprise star of a Dutch-made reality television show called *Outback Luke* in which he lassoed cattle while attractive girls vied for his attention. Luke makes a good living working in the offshore energy business, a seriously cashed-up greaser. Luke and Bill are off paragliding around Europe as I write, jumping off some Alpine escarpment and hitching a gentle ride across the thermals.

My aunt Mary collected me from Bill's house in Bright and we drove 500 kilometres east to the Gold Coast, then to Canberra. In all, we encountered no more than fifty other vehicles, some of them the massive lorries, known as road trains, that keep the outback supplied. We crossed mist-covered mountain ranges and huge, empty expanses of farmland which had been burned brown only months before but were now flooded. Along the humid, stormy beaches of the Gold Coast were scattered thousands of dead seabirds. I thought I was witnessing the consequences of some vast environmental catastrophe, but it was a natural phenomenon. These were short-tailed shearwaters, known locally as mutton birds. The shearwaters' sole breeding-grounds are the islands off south-east Australia. In the autumn, the birds make a 15,000 kilometre migration to their wintering grounds in the North Pacific, passing up the coast of Japan to reach Alaska. When spring comes, they fly south again, this time touching the coast of California before heading out across the Central Pacific, beating against the prevailing winds. By the time they approach Australia many of the birds are exhausted and fall into the sea. The birds I saw had died on the home stretch. It was just nature weeding out the weakest.

Back in the 1960s, Mary had done her nursing training then gone to New Zealand to work as a 'fifty-pound Pom'. She'd had a great time; she had been a member of the Wanganui Symphony Orchestra and had also loved the outdoors life. Like Bill, she felt at home, far from England; New Zealand and Australia seemed able to accommodate both her artistic and pragmatic sides without making her feel out of place. She subsequently moved to Canberra where she met Eric Hayes, the lithe little forester from Hutton Lowcross days. Eric had married one of the Florey daughters from Hutton and gone off to Australia to work for the Australian Forestry Commission; by the time he met Mary again he was divorced.

Mary and Eric went travelling together. She was going to take up a scholarship at the School of Nursing in Canberra when she discovered she was pregnant; so she ended up married to Eric and living at Pierce's Creek, the remote forestry station outside Canberra where Eric had worked since 1960, planting Monterey pines.

They were a funny double act, Mary and Eric. She was acute, bookish and musical; he was tough, reticent and seemingly dispassionate, though fiercely loyal. She had a stock of anecdotes to illustrate Eric's priorities. When she asked him what she should do in the event of a bush fire, he told her to 'get down that paddock and let my horses out'. She remembered trailing across the bush with Eric on a hot day, following him as he led a horse in foal. She herself was eight months pregnant and exhausted. Eric paused to water the horse at a creek: 'It does take it out of them,' he said.

Eric could do anything, fix anything and survive anything. When he cut himself open with a chainsaw he stitched the gash up with a sewing needle and thread. He never took the easy option and maybe that was what attracted her to him; or perhaps it was that he gave her good stories to tell. They had two children, David and Ruth, one dark, one fair, but Mary eventually 'shot through' – the Aussie term for running off – and moved back to Canberra in 1991. It was an amicable separation; Eric stayed at Pierce's Creek and the children shuttled between their parents. It was their home, that forestry station. There was a community; they had their horses and their freedom. Ruth had all sorts of animals. She even reared a wombat that Eric had cut from the pouch of its mother who had been hit by a car.

On my visit, Mary took me to see Eric, who was by then managing a farm outside Canberra – Pierce's Creek forestry station had been burned down in the bush fire of January 2003, which had almost destroyed Canberra. Eric was caught up in the middle of the disaster. It began as three spot-fires started through lightning strikes on the

9th January. At Pierce's Creek there was a fire-watching tower and after an electrical storm the foresters would be up the tower, anxiously scanning the bush. They saw the spot-fires and expected to be told to go and chip around them, as they usually did; if the vegetation was chipped away around a fire, it could be contained. On this occasion, the decision was taken that the fires were too far away and should be left to burn out the vegetation. 'It was a stupid decision,' Eric said to me. 'I still marvel at the stupidity of it.'

Within twenty-four hours, there were several big fires in the Namadgi Park to the west and other fires gobbled up the bush to the south. The flames converged in a ragged, monstrous fire-front twenty miles wide in places. The weather was hot and dry and hazy with brisk westerly winds. In the suburbs of Canberra, kangaroos piled in to escape the flames. All week the fires raged. Saturday the 18th was the worst day. At Pierce's Creek, which lay directly between the fire and Canberra, the men faced a fire-front ten miles wide. It swept through in the early morning.

'The temperature in there must have been a thousand degrees,' said Eric. 'The flames were towering above the trees, sparks shooting hundreds of feet into the air, and all those sparks were landing a mile in front and starting new fires. There was this terrible wind that came with the fire. It made an awful sound, groaning and howling, and in front of the fire came the radiant heat. God, it was awful. It cooked every living thing.'

He was driving through the smoke in his truck when he came across four kangaroos sitting in the road. They seemed poised to run but were immobile. He thought they might be dying, and rather than leave them to suffer he got an axe from the back of his pick-up and went to finish them off. But they were all dead already, just sitting there, like the inhabitants of Herculaneum or Pompeii, suffocated in an instant.

How do you survive a catastrophe like that? You can try to outrun the flames, but in this case there were showers of sparks that were starting a net of fires into which everything was running and there was a thick oily black smoke so you couldn't see a thing. Bush fires smell like nothing else: oily, acrid, bittersweet. You can try to defend your property – clear the ground around the house, stay indoors and hope that the fire will pass by, if it's not too big. But if the conditions are in its favour, absolutely nothing can stop the fire. By the time Eric and the other foresters had made sure that the residents had gone, they were trapped themselves. They parked up on the lee of a grass slope and saw the fire leap over their heads. Eric watched in horrified fascination as his life's work disappeared. There was a big pine, forty years old, one of the first ones he had planted; it was usually filled with birds. He saw it ripped out of the ground by a whirlwind created by the firestorm. Other trees just exploded. There was a hill, maybe 400 foot, covered with eucalyptus. The fire ran up the lower slopes; there was a pause and then a roar, a huge bang and a pillar of smoke that turned into a mushroom cloud. When the smoke cleared there was nothing living left, just the bare black hill. The eucalyptus trees had given off an oily vapour that had exploded. Eric watched his own house disappear in seconds.

The fires ran on to Canberra. The sprawling garden city was bathed in an eerie, yellow half-light, whipped by high hot winds that swirled choking dust and smoke. Flames ran up the suburban streets, and there they stopped, just yards short of the house that Mary was living in.

'Nothing but the city stopped it,' said Eric. 'It ran out of fuel. It had got so big it needed so much fuel to maintain its temperature. It's over when it's over, a fire like that. You don't put it out. It consumes itself.'

Remarkably, just four people died and 300 were injured. But more than 350 homes had been destroyed. What happened afterwards is a source of deep resentment. The state authorities promised to rebuild Pierce's Creek, then changed their minds and instead used the land to extend the Cotter Dam. My cousins David and Ruth were left homeless and angry. They function in the everyday world, but you can see that they belong elsewhere. In the city, they still move like people used to being outside. They are in a kind of exile.

Somehow, all our family have had to cast about for a home: we have found them and lost them, again and again. Nothing has come easily. I think of Robert, and all those appetites, all that food, booze, coffee, drugs and fags. He lived like Alice in Wonderland, taking this and taking that, blowing up and shrinking down, as he hoped he could make himself the right size to crawl through some keyhole into the proper space.

Where would he have been happy? One thing about Robert that his brothers and sisters can all agree on was that he loved his mother desperately, the more so because his father was so remote. He found it hard to leave her. She was home to him, a place within a person, where he felt all the indeterminate elements of his life could be resolved. She was herself full of contradictions, and they were his too: he was the product of those contradictions, the child she had instead of the life she felt she ought to have had. He belonged to her.

The Brooks children searched for a place to belong. If Robert found it so very much harder than the others, it was because his sense of a home was so undefined and then so final and forbidden. It had been buried with his mother in 1976. Ten years later, he had gone home to her.

19

SNOWDROPS

After twenty years of mild winters, the snow returned to Danby with a vengeance in 2009. Peter, Shelagh's husband, sent me some pictures of High Bramble Carr that rolled back time. I had forgotten how, up there, really thick snow still manages to suggest the outline of everything it covers, so this white world, sparkling with ice crystals under a blue sky, portrayed the curve and dip of known places, but it was as if the detail had all been eroded rather than covered over.

Further south, in Lincolnshire, my parents had some of the worst weather in the country, east coast weather like the moors, the first full blast of wind circulating in the Arctic or over Russia, and driving down the North Sea. A bit of winter snow was not unusual; but suddenly the gentle hills where my parents lived became ice-bound mountains, impassable to most cars. Their situation was isolated and difficult.

In the autumn of 2009, my father was diagnosed with oesophageal cancer. It had been suspected, but by the time the diagnosis was confirmed it was already late in the day for treatment. I think Dad knew from the start that he was in trouble. He talked about what he would do to the house the next spring, but inside, he doubted he would survive. I remember him sitting next to me under the cherry on the front lawn, by then cankered and dying back, with its leaves turning scarlet and falling. 'Bit of a bugger this,' he said, running his hand through his hair, in a familiar anxious gesture. He was scared, I could see, working out how to deal with the situation, whether to fight it or accept it. In the end, consciously or not, he seemed to begin preparing himself to die.

My mother on the other hand was utterly determined to live. She went about life with the same organising energy as before. The physical effects of the stroke became less obvious but she had to talk or her mouth would freeze up. Dad, meanwhile, was gradually closing down and had fewer and fewer words. It was like watching removal men empty a house. Bit by bit, the life vanished from him. He sat at the kitchen table for hours, hunched in some shapeless fleece jacket, reading and rereading the newspaper. After retiring from the RAF, he had struggled to find the correct costume in which to face the world. He had donated his RAF uniform to charity; the whites of the superb tennis player disappeared as his knees got creaky. His wardrobe was gradually invaded by a collection of baggy corduroy trousers and nondescript green or brown fleece jackets.

He shuffled around the place. Mum was upset that he seemed content to be shapeless and shabby, though she had in the past found it hard to live with a man who had been so sharply defined by arrogance. It was as if he had tried to make himself less of a sod, only to find that did not please her either. She missed the swagger he once had. He had been angry and wayward when they were young – there was no doubt he had been unfaithful and, oh God, his obsession with food and mealtimes: when my sister Mary was born Dad rewarded Mum with the gift of a deep-freeze. But we children noticed that he would never hear a bad word said about Mum. He depended utterly on her. There was a lingering awe in his feelings for her. I think that due to his own lack of self-esteem, he could never quite believe that she had married him. She, in turn, resented the maternal role in which he cast her, and never trusted her authority within the marriage.

The final scenes of their domestic stand-off were not unfamiliar to my mother. In Dad's illness, Mum relived both her mother's fury at her father's silence and her own exasperation at her mother's physical neediness. My father had become a combination of both George and Dorothy at their worst: a child's nightmare.

The funny thing was that immediately after the diagnosis, there had been a brief period when Dad had seemed elated, almost euphoric. For a couple of weeks, he was wise, serene and content. He had felt ill: maybe he had felt ill one way and another for many years. He had certainly felt wrong. Then he was diagnosed and treatment prescribed, so he thought that things would change. He would be cured and his life would change. The euphoria sprang from a case of mistaken identity; there was a metamorphosis about to occur, but it was not the one he anticipated. Within a few months, that truth seemed to have sunk in.

I went by to see my parents regularly. They lived just twenty minutes away. One December evening, I called my mother to say I would bring the three children across to see Dad.

'Oh good,' she said. 'That cheers him up. He comes awake. Puts on a show for the visitors. Then flumph. Flumph.' She was scared and angry with him for dying, and angry that when people came he put on his show and then collapsed when they went out the door: she was scared about what would happen next. My mother was chewing gum at the time: it helped loosen her jaw so she could speak. She was tense with emotion much of the time; when I spoke to her on the phone I could hear this furious chewing noise.

I remember that we turned up in the dusk; my mother was outside, locking sheds, posed against the white painted doors, shrunk in the gloom like a child turned to the wall for a game of hide and seek. She was wearing a woollen hat and the left side of her face was drawn up.

'He's not well, you know. He's just sitting there. He'll jolly up when you come in. Then afterwards, he'll just flumph.'

I hadn't seen my father for ten days. He was sitting at the kitchen table, facing both doors. He dragged himself around the room, was thinner, more tired and round-shouldered. He slumped forwards or lolled backwards as if to relieve some pressure. His face had a glossy, bloodless pallor and shadows seemed to float on the surface. With the weight loss, he looked more and more like his father: the rigidity around the jawline, the enigmatic smile that was not a smile and a gleaming eye.

He was genuinely pleased to see me. 'Haven't seen you for a while,' he said, giving me one of his big hugs. Hanging by the fireplace were two little signs: 'Gone to feed the chickens' and 'Working in the garden'. My son, Ralph, then two years old, liked to climb up to get them and have my mother repeat the words written on them. Dad made me a cup of coffee. It was awful, made in the cafetière but lukewarm and thick with grey solids. He had forgotten to boil the kettle. We talked about cricket. Virender Sehwag, the Indian opener had scored 284 in a day; I'd seen the highlights.

'So you said, so you said,' he murmured, and nodded and nodded.

We both watched Ralph. There seemed to be little to say, a horrible sag in the atmosphere. He didn't want to be cheered or changed and seemed mistrustful of laughter. I gave him a tin of Roses chocolates. 'I can only eat Belgian,' he said. 'They melt in the mouth.'

'You could try letting these melt.' I suggested, slightly exasperated yet aware of how unfair this was. 'They have soft centres.'

He nodded, grim. 'I'll see. I'll try.'

My parents had just travelled to London to see my actress sister Lucy in a play in the West End. 'It was very good,' said Mum. 'Very good.'

'Are you going to tell him about the journey?' asked Dad.

'Well you can if you want to. I don't know why you'd want to . . .'

He looked at her, annoyed. 'Well, it wasn't very smooth. Bloody awful trains. We upgraded to first class but it didn't make any difference as we didn't get any free coffee or tea.'

'It wasn't that bad, Tim.'

'It wasn't smooth.'

After the play Lucy had taken them to Sheekey's fish restaurant. 'I had a lobster bisque that I could manage,' said Dad, leaning back and pulling a face of strange self-aggrandisement. 'And some ice-cream. It was called

Sheehies.' He pronounced the name as if it was Irish. 'Sheehies.'

'No, Tim! No!' said Mum diving in as if he had tried to overtake a lorry on a blind bend, a note of utter panic in her voice and her eyes flashing warning signs that this man was not to be trusted: 'It was Sheekies. Sheeekeees!'

When I was ten or so, I used to hang around my parents as they sat at the kitchen table after a meal. It was then the rows would often begin to build, so I would put a cloth over my arm and pretend to be a waiter, trying to make them laugh, negotiating between them. All their children tried in similar ways to make the grown-ups grow up; but again and again they returned to this mutually compulsive stand-off. We would have approved if Mum had simply walked away: we hated to see her unhappy. She could draw and ride horses and Dad would be perfectly OK living above a pub somewhere. We wanted our parents to separate; it was something that, as children, we discussed. But they went on and on this way as if neither of them possessed the confidence to face the world alone – as if they had taken each other's confidence and could not give it back.

With Dad dying, the game was running its course. It all felt wrong, but there was nothing I could do. We carried on going through the motions. I helped Dad with the winter ritual of putting up the double glazing on the kitchen window. He insisted on doing some things, finding a step ladder and carrying the smaller piece of glass through from the stables. The exertion left him completely breathless.

'He feels unwell now,' my mother said later, in a plain

236

statement of fact, saying what he could not. 'Now he feels really unwell. But he won't talk to me about it.'

People survive cancer, but it takes a great deal of determination. Dad, in his passivity, seemed to have made a decision to die. He reacted badly to his chemo sessions, but carried on drinking in between and even having the odd smoke. The blood transfusions he was given perked him up, but he so disliked hospital appointments that he would put them off if he could and even managed, gleefully, to argue his way out of the radiotherapy session that had been prescribed.

My father had to be driven across the Wolds to these hospital appointments in Lincoln. Despite her stroke, my mother was driving again without any difficulty, so she took him when she could, but I often drove him or picked him up afterwards. We would talk then, about the landscape we were driving through.

Whatever passing regrets I had about buying that house in Lincolnshire, it had enabled me to be close to my parents and to fill in the gaps in our relationship. I had come to know Dad a lot better, and with that, any resentment of the past had faded. We had also found a way to talk.

I realised that Dad was at heart a country boy. He grew up in the sunken lanes and sultry woodlands of a long-gone Devon, acquiring all the knowledge that was then considered essential for an adolescent, about birds and butterflies, mushrooms and trees. I wrote about trees. That interest in the world outside me had helped me put my own troubles in context, and now it gave us things to chat about. Dad had an old-fashioned relationship with trees – more matey than mystic. From climbing them in shorts he acquired skinned knees and a wonderful collection of birds' eggs, about which he felt guilty later in life. But those were different times, when there seemed to be plenty of everything for young hands to grab on to. I liked it when he told stories about his childhood.

He loved the grain and colour of fine wood, particularly walnut, a favourite tree which he had a knack for spotting in hedgerows and overgrown Victorian gardens, where big old walnuts often lurk forgotten, their leaves, at a distance, not so very different from the fingers of the ash. Walnuts often have gloriously proportioned, athletic forms and Dad was a top games player. He loved the sensual aspects of the tree, the aromatic leaves and the nuts, which reminded him of Italy. His home-grown walnuts had a dense, faintly bitter, sweetly oily taste, a flavour so close to diesel fumes it ought to have been repugnant, yet bizarrely it complemented everything from ripe cheese to milk chocolate.

Dad's passion for walnuts inevitably brought him into conflict with the grey squirrels, which stripped the bark and fruit from his trees. Their battles over the walnut at the bottom of his garden said much about his stubborn sense of proprietorship. It was a game, but a deadly serious game. In the RAF he scored highly in air gunnery and he remained an excellent shot. By sniping from a bedroom window he was able to dispatch many squirrels, but no sooner would he be settling down under the cherry tree with a cup of tea, than the irate chattering of the latest grey marauder would echo through the garden.

He would run his hand through his hair with that nervous gesture and smile ruefully. Deep down, he hated the feeling that something was stealing what he felt to be rightfully his: the war of the walnut tree became a way of articulating and making light of some personal wound, the origins of which lay elsewhere, far in the obscure past, in what his own parents had never delivered.

It was true that he could not talk about himself. It was all a mass of swirling things in there. Contemplation of it made him gloomy. Probably my mother forced him too much to consider that incoherence, to neither's satisfaction. He could not express himself directly. But if you listened closely to what he said, you would often find that there were hidden metaphors, analogies for what he felt or thought.

The dark days of winter made him gloomy and he looked eagerly for the first signs of the turning year; yellow aconites in the shrubberies and snowdrops under the naked trees. The day before he died, as I drove him to hospital for another futile transfusion, he asked me how the snowdrops were doing in my woods. 'Mmm, slowly,' I replied. He nodded, his face impassive: 'I shall dig a few up and put them in a pot on my windowsill to make them come out sooner.' A moment later my heart froze as I realised that he was quietly telling me he did not have very long. I think that in his animal way, he knew it was time. He died the next morning.

Mum survived. Though she did not necessarily feel it, she was always the stronger: she found reasons to live. She had things she loved doing: she had a rigorous domestic routine, children, grandchildren and animals that needed her attention. In retrospect, she saw what a desperate battle those last few months had been, how my father had effectively demurred and bowed out.

She put snowdrops on his coffin.

20

REMAINS

In August, eighteen months after my father's funeral, Shelagh told me that Ilsa Kenney, former landlady of the Fox and Hounds, had died. I had seen Ilsa a few months before and she had been on good form. After leaving Danby, she had moved to Northallerton and had become very involved with charity work; she kept her looks, and when I saw her, had a much younger boyfriend. When she became ill, she had returned to Danby, where her daughters lived, so they could look after her for the last stretch.

I took Mum up to the funeral in Danby Methodist chapel, a handsome, light place, where Dorothy had often played the piano for the Dalesmen choir. We sat next to Brenda Tindall from Rowantree Farm, who had not seen Mum for thirty-five years but recognised her. It was the same outside the service and again in the party that was held at the Fox and Hounds – people remembered her, and talked as if George and Dorothy were still up the road.

The Fox and Hounds has passed through several hands since my grandparents' day: there is a new bar, more dining facilities, more rooms, and loos that no longer freeze solid in winter. But the old granite fireplace is still there with its scallops and interlocking hoops, and the pub still feels much the same, thick-walled and snug and enduring. It is still a popular locals pub, as well as a summer drop-in for visitors. From the top rooms you can look over the dale and watch the skies shift from grey to blue and back. The smell of peat and heather trickles down from the moors.

In the bar, after Ilsa's funeral, I bumped into Harry, Shelagh Gray's first husband, the one who came along after the circus lad. Harry was an ace mechanic who longed to fly, another lad who loved the RAF. I recognised him in the Fox from a picture Shelagh showed me of him as a young man, sitting with a pint. More than thirty years on he looked just the same, slight and boyish, with a mop of hair, almost ageless: even the pint seemed untouched. Harry remembered my grandparents and my mother, but he remembered my father, too.

'Didn't he fly those Lightnings?' he asked, his eyes flashing with excitement and awe. 'Just like a rocket. Nothing like them, ever.'

The past remained alive for both my parents.

Ilsa had been cremated. I asked Liz, her daughter, if they would be putting her mother's ashes down in Danby graveyard with John's? She said they were thinking about it, but her father had enjoyed thirty-five years' respite from Ilsa, so why spoil it now? They would hold on to the ashes for a while. Actually, they still had Ilsa's mother's ashes somewhere, and those of her aunt, or was it her sister?

The problem with cremation is that if you don't get

rid of the ashes straight away, then you can dither for ages about what seems to be the most appropriate place, about what is the rightful home for someone's remains – about who they belonged to, or where. Put someone in the earth and they are just there, rightly or wrongly: rooted, buried and gone. But the flames seem to bring them back to life.

This is true of my father, who was cremated and was supposed to be scattered more than a year ago, but is still in an urn in the loft where he framed prints and drank, while we hold occasional discussions as to the ideal place for him, something that will provide the living with a sense of closure. It is also true of my uncle Robert; Bill intended to scatter him in a favourite wood in Tasmania, but never got round to it. For years Robert sat on Bill's mantelpiece, until Rose eventually brought him back to England. Now he is in a garage outside York, awaiting further orders. Rose thinks that we should all have a scoop of him. One is always looking for the correct way to close the past: it can't be articulated, so we hang on to the dead until they belong with the living. The ashes become possessions, carried around from home to home, always alive. All over the world, I expect it is the same: ashes stored in cupboards and chests and lofts and garden sheds all indicative of how persistent the past is in us, how necessary, how beloved, and how we cannot ever say quite what we mean.

Later, when I walked with my mother up Danby Rigg, the heather was just coming into flower. In amongst it, that sea of purple broke down into its foaming constituent elements, a mass of colours, mauve and white and brown and the lipstick pink of bell heather. It was as much a garden as a landscape. There were sheep up on the moors again: the Dawnay Estate and the farmers have made a start at trying to claw back some of the grazing, though many of the paths and views on Danby Rigg are still overgrown.

Grouse scattered from the heather around us, calling 'go-back, go-back, go-back,' telling us not to trespass on their land. In fact, the heather is their world; it was created as their habitat. One forgets that the late summer, purple sheen of the moorland is not a natural occurrence, but the consequence of hard-nosed decisions taken by land-owners in the nineteenth century, who set about extending the heather habitat for grouse shooting. The moors were once a more varied mixture of forest, scrub, bog and cotton grass. Grouse eat only young heather so the land-owners cut the trees, burned the scrub, and closed the land.

They wanted profitable sport. It was never their inten-tion to create anything marvellous in the moorland scenery, but there it is, as far as the eye can see: a glorious gift of greed. It is laughable: you can fret endlessly throughout life, searching for the right gesture, the correct word or picture, worrying about your motives and how you wish to be remembered. In the end, the best of intentions seem to create havoc. Then there is this – thirty miles of glorious purple effluent, beauty as a waste product. Pragmatism and industry have produced a work of art that no artist could ever conceive.

ACKNOWLEDGEMENTS

This book would not have been possible without considerable help from my family. I am particularly grateful to my mother, Mu Cohu, for her courage and candidness, my sister Lucy for her perspective, and, yet again, for the unwavering support of my brother John. My aunts, Rose and Mary, sifted the past for me and my uncle Bill helped me in more ways than I could have hoped.

I owe a great deal to the people of Danby; in particular Shelagh Mernagh, who opened many boxes and doors, and her husband Peter who took such an evocative cover image; Brenda and Bob Tindall; Enid Raw; Herbert and Annie Sutcliffe and the members of the Court Leet; the late Ilsa McNicol-Kenney, and her daughters Jane and Liz; Eric Hayes, and Malcolm East.

My account of Bob Robinson's time at Ainthorpe House draws on his *History of Danby,* privately published in 1990. I am grateful to his children Susanna, Eddie and Louise for their contributions. Thanks to Charles Hart for supplying a retreat when it was needed; and to the silver bird, whose song was always audible, no matter how faint.

I am profoundly grateful for the support of The Royal Literary Fund, which gave me a grant at a critical time in the writing of this book. Thanks also to all at Rogers

Coleridge & White and Chatto; especially to Juliet Brooke for her acute questions and – above all – to Clara Farmer, for her faith.

Will Cohu, December 2011